Read,
Reflect,
Write

Read, Reflect, Write

The Elements of

✓ Flexible Reading
✓ Fluent Writing
✓ Independent Learning

CARMEN COLLINS
Rutgers University

Prentice-Hall, Inc., Englewood Cliffs, New Jersey 07632

Library of Congress Cataloging in Publication Data

Collins, Carmen.
    Read, reflect, write.

    Includes bibliographical references and index.
        I. Study, Method of.   2. Language arts (Higher)
I. Title.
LB2395.C623   1984   378'.1702812   83-13700
ISBN 0-13-753558-9

© 1984 by Carmen Collins

Printed in the United States of America

10   9   8   7   6   5   4   3   2   1

Editorial/production supervision and
    interior design: Virginia Cavanagh Neri
Cover design: 20/20 Services, Inc., Mark Berghash
Manufacturing buyer: Harry Baisley

ISBN 0-13-753558-9

Prentice-Hall International, Inc., *London*
Prentice-Hall of Australia Pty. Limited, *Sydney*
Editora Prentice-Hall do Brasil, Ltda., *Rio de Janeiro*
Prentice-Hall Canada Inc., *Toronto*
Prentice-Hall of India Private Limited, *New Delhi*
Prentice-Hall of Japan, Inc., *Tokyo*
Prentice-Hall of Southeast Asia Pte. Ltd., *Singapore*
Whitehall Books Limited, *Wellington, New Zealand*

Contents

six   Re-Reading/Writing: Critical Thinking   78

seven   Using Techniques Taught   98

Quick Reference: *Read, Reflect, Write* Strategies   111

Appendix   126

Index   157

Preface

Read, Reflect, Write is a textbook which truly integrates *instruction* in Reading and Writing. It combines college level reading and writing in one practical handbook for the mature learner who must master the advanced skills needed for reading complicated textbooks and writing clear, coherent reports and papers. Throughout, it addresses the student as reader and writer *in one*, helping him or her to move easily among the roles of reader, writer, and thinker. Moreover, it helps students witness, first hand, the interactions among these roles in their own learning. Reinforcement occurs as students practice newly learned techniques by applying them to their textbooks and assignments in other subjects.

Based on the latest research into the integral relationship between reading and writing, *Read, Reflect, Write* bridges the gap between theory and practice by providing students with powerful metacognitive learning strategies which are known to work. While the book takes students through a process in which reading, writing, and thinking are integrated and interactive, it takes both new and experienced instructors through a unique curriculum model which may be adapted to the varying levels and needs of students.

HOW TO USE THIS BOOK

Read, Reflect, Write may be used as a primary or supplementary text. It will complement subject textbooks, handbooks, or readers. It is intended for use in college reading courses, writing classes, study skills workshops, communications skills, English as a second language and adult basic education courses, or in learning laboratories where students are tutored or expected to work independently.

This volume may also be used with a primary text in the social sciences, psychology, and history, as well as in certain science, vocational, technological, and computer science courses where informational reading and report writing are required.

Read, Reflect, Write follows a developmental and cumulative sequence and is best used in the order it is written. The first three chapters prepare students for the combined reading/writing process by getting them to read and write immediately while monitoring their own progress.

Chapter One, *The Independent Learner*, places the responsibility for learning with the student. The techniques of analyzing one's own learning style, monitoring one's progress, and increasing one's usable vocabulary demonstrate to students how *conscious reflection* can strengthen the learning process.

Chapter Two, *The Flexible Reader*, discusses three different reading modes for flexibility, shows students how to calculate their reading rate and monitor reading habits. A daily program of pleasure reading, with a short written response, increases reading strengths and assures students they *can* become flexible readers.

Chapter Three, *The Fluent Writer*, emphasizes process and attempts to establish the habits of daily writing and reflection. The chapter discusses three different modes for effective writing, shows students how each mode is used for different purposes, and assures them they can become fluent writers.

Chapters Four, Five, and Six constitute the core of the reading/writing approach. The diagram, *Interrelationships Among the Practices of Analytical Reading, Thinking, Writing* describes visually the theory upon which the *Read, Reflect, Write* method is based. It shows how the practices of reading, writing, and thinking are related in each of three phases: Preparation, Discernment, and Evaluation.

Interrelationships Among the Practices of Analytical Reading, Thinking, Writing

	READING	THINKING	WRITING
I. Pre-Reading/Writing (Preparation)	**Skimming:** Understanding Central Ideas	**Literal Understanding:** What is the Main Message?	**Free Writing:** Generating Ideas for Main Message
II. Reading/Writing (Discernment)	**Moderate Reading Rate:** Making Sense of Details; Making Inferences	**Inferential Reasoning:** Do supporting details substantiate Main Message? What are unstated ideas? Implications	**Focused Writing:** Substantiating Main Message with Specific Supporting Details, Implications
III. Re-Reading/Writing *(Evaluation)*	**Deliberate Reading:** Evaluating Information; Assessing Implications	**Critical Thinking:** What is the text's Purpose, Organization, Effectiveness, Implication?	**Formal Writing:** Rethinking Reordering Reorganizing Reevaluating Application

PREPARATION

Chapter Four, *Pre-Reading/Writing* (Literal Thinking), covers the *Preparation* stage for reading/writing. This stage includes the kinds of thinking associated with skimming a text to comprehend central ideas, thesis, and conclusion, and skimming the mind to generate central ideas, thesis, and conclusion for an original essay. In practice, the reader/writer moves quickly to gain a preliminary view of a written text, to make preliminary decisions about an original essay, and to get a central perspective on a continuum of events. The preparation phase helps students better understand another author's main message and to focus on their own main message when writing.

DISCERNMENT

Chapter Five, *Reading/Writing* (Inferential Reasoning), covers the *Discernment* phase, or the close reading of a text and focused writing of a first draft. This stage deals with understanding hierarchies of ideas, seeing relationships, making inferences, and having an awareness of an order of central and supporting ideas. In practice, the reader/writer moves at a moderate pace to take a closer look at a text and to write a first draft of an essay or paper. The discernment phase develops inferential reasoning competencies while helping students see relationships and levels among their own ideas.

EVALUATION

Chapter Six, *Re-Reading/Writing* (Critical Thinking), covers the critical rereading of a text and the evaluative rewriting of a draft. This stage deals with the clarification of levels, purpose, order, form, intent, and sequence of ideas. In practice, the reader/writer moves more deliberately to verify meaning and intent of an author's text, and to clearly recombine original ideas into coherent wholes. The evaluation phase helps students understand how another author combines multiple ideas into a coherent whole as they, themselves, reorder, rearrange, and rewrite ideas with growing coherence and clarity.

Chapter Seven, *Using Techniques Taught,* reviews and reinforces the principles of the preceding chapters through their application to writing the research paper and taking essay examinations. Students use outside sources of information from both the textbook's appendix and the library to write a researched paper. In a similar way, students apply reading/writing techniques to better understand and respond to essay questions on examinations. Feedback and discussion with classmates make the complex tasks of research and test taking easier to handle.

The *Read, Reflect, Write* process requires time for practice and reflection and best proceeds at a leisurely pace. However, it may be possible, under certain conditions, to allow one week only for each chapter, then to repeat the reading/writing sequences of Chapters Four, Five, and Six for each subsequent assignment using supplemental reading materials. Indeed, the use of supplemental readings (essays and textbooks) is strongly recommended.

TEXTBOOK READINGS

Readings on the single subject of *sleep* have been chosen for a number of reasons: first, for the universality of the topic; second, to show students how writers may explore one subject in various ways; and third, to provide a resource for reading assignments and the research paper.

ACTIVITIES

Read, Reflect, Write includes both *Independent* and *Group Activities* at the end of each chapter. Independently, students are assigned reading or rereading and are asked questions on which to reflect and write. Group work includes questions for discussion in class or in small groups, whichever the instructor prefers.

APPLICATION

Application is a crucial section. Research shows that when relationships and connections are pointed out to students, transfer of learning is more likely to occur. Therefore, in this section, connections are made between strategies taught and their application to reading and writing in other subjects.

In summary, *Read, Reflect, Write* takes students in planned, developmental steps, from literal thinking and free writing to critical thinking and formal writing while helping them become metacognitively aware of what is happening in their own learning. Hopefully this knowledge will encourage students to value the most important and intrinsic reward—better understanding.

Writing this textbook has been a thoroughly enjoyable experience and although it is not possible to thank everyone who has affected the work, I wish to thank my colleagues at Rutgers University for their support and their friendship. Many thanks must go to my students whose abilities and progress never cease to amaze me. Special thanks go to Prentice-Hall's Bill Oliver, Phil Miller, Ginny Neri, and Lisa Femmel. I also wish to thank the insightful reviewers for their kind and helpful advice all along the way: Gail Z. Benchener, De Anza Community College; Douglas Butturff, University of Central Arkansas; Patricia Grignon, Saddleback Community College; Kris O'Harra, Chemeketa Community College; Regina Rinderer, Southern Illinois University; and Jacqueline Viggiano and Patricia Waelder, Onondaga Community College.

Most important, I would like to thank my family: my daughter Marie for her caring and careful reading of the manuscript, my son Paul for his support and encouragement, and my husband Bob for his reading and rereading of the manuscript and for his patience, love, and unfailing wit.

Finally, I am overwhelmingly grateful to the technology which made possible the *wondrous* word processor.

Carmen Collins

Read,
Reflect,
Write

Introduction

As college students, you are expected to read many textbooks and to write clear and concise examinations and term papers. Three essential skills must be mastered if you are to succeed. First, you will have to read, understand, and remember many different kinds of information for your courses; second, you will be required to write assignments, reports, and term papers; and third, you will be taking tests, quizzes, and examinations regularly. Reading, writing, and thinking are indeed the *tools of the trade* in college. Despite your varied experiences in reading, writing, and thinking, you will need to learn new strategies to deal with the volume of work, the more complex subject matter, and the additional responsibilities that come with the freedom of managing assignments and deadlines on your own.

The amount of reading, writing, and thinking in college is demanding. You will be taking four or five courses and may have to read at least two or three books for each. In addition, you will be using the library regularly. Even if you breezed through other books, you will find that a larger portion of your time in college will be consumed by reading. Term papers are expected in many courses. Even if you never wrote a term paper or a report, you will spend a good deal of your time preparing for or actually writing them. Tests are inevitable; some will be short answer or

1

multiple-choice types; others will be essay examinations. Overall, your work and study time in college can be a full-time job.

The subject matter of your new textbooks, term papers, and tests may be both new and complex. Writing assignments frequently require research and time for reflection. Examinations often compel you to understand and remember both facts and concepts. You will find that you have to work harder to learn certain concepts, while other subjects will be *naturals* and you will expend less effort absorbing them. Most important, college work is stimulating; certain subjects and writing assignments will intrigue and excite you into thinking about your life's work and your future.

Finally, no one will be around to remind you of your assignments, to see that you are doing your work, or to monitor your progress. In other words, you are on your own. You and you alone are responsible for using time wisely, for dealing with the required reading assignments, for handing in reports and papers promptly. To survive in college, you have to become an independent learner.

In *Read, Reflect, Write*, you will discover how to read efficiently and understand large volumes of information, how to write fluent, clear reports and papers, how to use reading and writing to master the art of test taking, how to become an independent learner. *Read, Reflect, Write* can promise that you will learn, because all of the lessons have been tested many times, and students, like yourself, were first to recognize these highly successful strategies. Only the most successful have been included in this book. You are in college because you have chosen to learn; therefore, *you will learn*. Everything in this textbook is geared to your success. The method has worked for others, and it will work for you.

WHY THE METHOD WORKS

The *Read, Reflect, Write* method works because it is based on solid educational principles that recognize the important relationship between reading and writing. It has provided students with numerous opportunities to understand this crucial relationship and to practice reading and writing as though one were part of the other. Actually, you cannot have one without the other. All reading originates with writing, and all writing, if it is to be communicated, must be read. In other words, reading *is* writing, and writing *is* reading.

All the uses of language—speaking, listening, reading, and writing—are interrelated. Try to recall learning, as a child, to speak and to listen. Chances are you cannot remember learning to listen, and you probably learned to speak with little fanfare, particularly if you come from a large family and you were not the first born. When you went to school, you were taught the *visual* counterparts of speaking and listening; reading became the visible way of listening, while writing became the visible way of speaking. You were taught, in effect, that it is possible to use an *invisible* aspect of language (listening, speaking) when your audience is present (or visible), but that you need a *visible* language when you cannot see your audience. Logical, isn't it?

It is equally logical that the same alphabet and similar word ordering comprise all our uses of language. Listening, speaking, reading, writing, and yes, even thinking, for the most part, occur in our native tongue. Can you imagine learning to read and write without the ability to listen and speak? People who are born deaf, who never hear the sounds of language, rarely learn to speak with the clarity of a hearing person. However, because the connection between all uses of language is so strong, many persons who have hearing losses later in life learn to speak, read, and write simply because, at one time, they were able to listen. You who have the gifts of language soon will look at reading and writing in an exciting new way.

Read, Reflect, Write merges the two processes of reading and writing for you, shows you the similarities between them, and points to new ways of using reading for improving your writing, and, thanks to recent research findings, shows how writing can improve your reading. You will be learning college-level techniques in reading and writing simultaneously; you will be both reader and writer, *in one*. You will learn that writers and readers perform different, yet similar, tasks: a writer *makes* meaning *with* words, and a reader *takes* meaning *from* words. Both writer and reader, however, use the same ingredients—words, which are shaped into ideas through thinking, and thoughts, which are preserved on paper for reflection.

Since you, as a college student, are constantly required to perform as both reader and writer, you must move freely between the two roles, gleaning ideas with new understanding and generating ideas with new fluency. When you read a chapter, you will use writing skills to increase your comprehension; when you write a term paper, you will use reading techniques to improve your composition.

Each time you practice a given *Read, Reflect, Write* technique, you reinforce skills which eventually will become part of your automatic response system. Gradually, old habits will be replaced with newer and more efficient ways of working and studying, and you will wonder how you ever got by without the *Read, Reflect, Write* approach.

The combination of effective reading and competent writing will help you become not only a better student, but an independent learner as well—talents you can take with you into your life's work—proficiencies you will use to ensure continuous learning. But now, being a college student means that *you are both reader and writer*. So, this book is all about *you*.

one

The Independent Learner

To prepare for this chapter, think about the way you learn. How do you best collect information? How do you organize and process ideas? Consider the steps you follow when solving a problem or arriving at a decision. Chances are your method of gaining knowledge follows a pattern or style of learning. Jot down all your immediate perceptions about the way you learn.

As you reflect and write about your personal mode of learning, try to include answers to the following questions: Do I learn best alone or when interacting with others? Do I learn best by listening, watching, or reading? Do I like to read instruction manuals, or do I prefer to learn by *doing* or experiencing, through a hands-on approach? Do I approach a task systematically or randomly? What strategies do I use for remembering? Do I tend to look at objects and situations as wholes, or do I see their separate parts? Do I learn best from verbal explanations, lectures, and talks, or from visual descriptions, diagrams, and charts? Would I rather have someone explain a problem, or do I prefer to try to figure it out myself? How do I approach a reading task or a writing assignment?

Your awareness of learning styles will provide clues to why you excel in one area of study and struggle with another. It will also help you recognize other people's styles of learning. Studies of young children show that learning styles develop early in life as ways of responding to the environment. Although there are no right or wrong ways of responding to the environment, some responses are more effective than others. When a response does not work effectively, you may have to analyze the situation to determine how to revise it. That is why familiarity with different learning styles, even if you use some and not others, may provide the insight you need for understanding a subject or situation. Trying new learning styles will prove that you *can* add variety to your personal learning practices, which, in turn, will add to your available strategies for gaining new knowledge.

WHAT YOU CAN EXPECT FROM THIS CHAPTER

The purpose of this chapter is to help you become an independent learner. You will find that there are different ways of learning a subject, just as there are different ways of approaching a task. This chapter introduces you to specific strategies for seeing written matter from different perspectives. Included also are techniques such as the *Textbook Checklist, Reflections after Class, Building a Better Vocabulary*, and the *Personal Vocabulary File*—all geared to putting you in charge of your own learning—the first step to becoming an independent learner.

WHAT IS AN INDEPENDENT LEARNER?

An independent learner is one who takes personal responsibility for his or her learning. Students who become independent learners tend to learn quickly, learn more, and retain what they learn longer than students who sit in class, arms folded, with attitudes that say, "Teach me, I dare you."

Studies have shown time and again that teaching does not ensure learning. Learning is possible only when an individual makes the decision to learn. The most competent instructor cannot teach a student who chooses not to learn. As a student, you have the freedom to choose; you also have the opportunity to improve your learning techniques and to become an independent learner.

CONTRASTS BETWEEN DEPENDENT AND INDEPENDENT LEARNING

After a particularly intense lecture in psychology, a group of students discusses the difficulties of managing time and organizing notes for the complex lecture. All but one student agree to form a study group to discuss psychology lectures, compare notes, and review for examinations. The nonjoiner remarks, "We shouldn't have to spend so much extra time on one subject. I allot a certain portion of my time for psychology and that's it. The instructor's job is to make the information clear. I shouldn't have to spend hours figuring out what the lecture means." The student walks away from the group. *Who are the dependent or independent learners?*

It would appear that the student moving away from the group is the independent one. Going off on one's own *seems* independent, but that may not be so. The term *independent learner* does not necessarily mean *lone* learner. For our purposes, independence means standing on one's own, not leaning on another person or making someone else responsible for one's progress—in this case, taking responsibility for one's own learning. Independent learners may derive equal satisfaction from group endeavors and solitary work. Most important, they freely choose either to interact with others or to work alone. Whatever the choice, independent learners prefer to rely on their own resources. Forming a study group is one resourceful way of taking responsibility for one's own learning.

HOW TO BECOME AN INDEPENDENT LEARNER

Another way of taking responsibility for your own learning is by looking at something from a new or different perspective. Each time you gain a new perspective, new learning occurs. Throughout this book, you will be looking at print, or textual material, from the perspective of both a reader and a writer. The reader/writer perspective brings a text's organization and meaning into focus through its emphasis on clear communication. Most attempts at communication, whether written or spoken, have three parts: a beginning, a middle, and an ending. Looking at beginnings, middles, and endings provides you with another perspective on language use.

LOOKING AT BEGINNINGS, MIDDLES, AND ENDINGS

Aside from helping us find our place in a text, beginnings, middles, and endings have specific purposes. An advertising man described the purposes of beginnings, middles, and endings best when he said, "Tell them what you are going to say [Beginnings]. Say it [Middles]. Tell them what you have said [Endings]."

Tell Them What You Are Going to Say

The job of the *beginning* is twofold. First, it introduces or prepares the reader for what is to come; second, it attempts to capture the reader's attention and interest.

The beginning of a book is called an introduction, a foreword, or a preface. If no formal beginning is used, the table of contents introduces the subject matter, and introductory chapters prepare the reader. In an essay, the introductory paragraphs frequently contain a *thesis* statement in which the author tells what the piece will be about. In some cases, a thesis is not stated outright; instead it is suggested or implied. In magazine articles, the introduction is called a *lead* and frequently contains a thesis, or, as one writer described it, a billboard paragraph, with much the same function as a road sign, in that it tells you where you are headed. As you can see, somewhere in the beginning of most kinds of writing, the writer prepares the reader for what is to come.

No amount of preparation will keep a reader reading unless the beginning captures attention or interest. One way to capture attention is to plant a question in the reader's mind. As a reader, you will read on if the beginning of a piece makes you ask, When?, Where?, Who?, How?, or Why? As a writer, you will have to put yourself in the reader's place. All the beginning strategies mentioned here are described at length in later chapters. For now, try to read as a writer and write as a reader, making an attempt to see print from both perspectives at the same time.

Say It

The job of the *middle* is to continue, expand, and support the promise of the beginning, while at the same time laying the groundwork for the conclusion or ending. The middle, or body, portions of print material contain the bulk of the information, and more often than not are longer than either the beginning or ending of a particular piece. The middle is also the link between the introduction and the conclusion, lending support to both the beginning and the ending. Middles will be discussed at length in later chapters so, for now, as reader/writer, remember that when there is no relationship between the beginning, middle, and ending of a text, something went wrong, either with the piece of writing or with the writer's sense of what he or she meant to say.

Tell Them What You Have Said

The job of an ending is to summarize, conclude, or to confirm facts which were introduced earlier in a piece of writing. In textbooks, endings may be labeled as summaries or may appear as questions at the ends of chapters. If the ending of a text is missing, the reader will sense it and become dissatisfied. Try reading an essay or chapter without completing the last few pages or paragraphs; you will feel "left up in the air," so to speak, and that is how your reader will feel if you write without thinking about your ending or conclusion. Endings will be discussed in detail later. For now, to use two well-known cliches, think of endings as *coming full circle* or *tying up loose ends*.

Watch for beginnings, middles, and endings as you read and write. When you recognize this magic threesome, you will see them everywhere in print and on television. Indeed, you will soon begin to *hear* beginnings, middles, and endings in television and radio reports, in the conversations of others, and in your own conversations with friends. Remember, tell them what you are going to say, say it, then tell them what you have said.

FIGURE 1-1   Beginnings, Middles, Endings

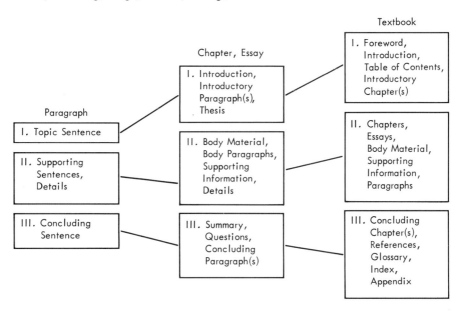

COMPARING TEXTBOOK, CHAPTER, ESSAY, PARAGRAPH

Figure 1-1 illustrates the similarities and differences among beginnings, middles, and endings of paragraph, essay, chapter, and textbook. The smallest unit in the group is the paragraph. Notice how paragraphs are the building blocks of the essay and chapter, while chapters and essays become the building blocks of the book.

Read Figure 1-1 in two different ways. First, look at it vertically (each column, from top to bottom), then look at it horizontally (across, as though no lines were drawn). Read across: Paragraph I, then Chapter I, Essay I, and Textbook I, etc. Do the same for II and III.

Now read the blank chart, Figure 1-2. Look at it vertically, then horizontally, as you looked at the completed chart. *Reflect* on the blank chart, considering carefully, the headings *One Day, A Meaningful Period, My Life.* Do you see any relationship between the sizes of the boxes on the charts and the amounts of time which the titles might encompass? Think about the titles *One Day, A Meaningful Period, My Life* and prepare to fill in the blanks on the chart in the following way.

For *One Day* think of a specific day. How did it begin, develop, and end? Write one sentence each to describe the beginning, middle, and ending of that day.

FIGURE 1-2   Beginnings, Middles, Endings

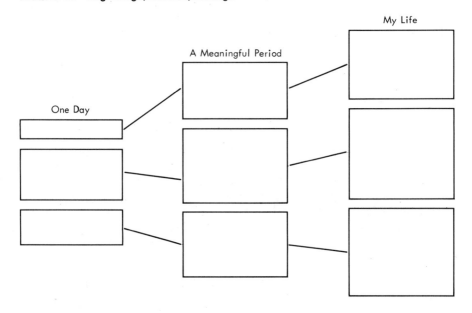

For *A Meaningful Period* think of an event in your life which continued over an extended period of time. How did the period begin? Did you meet someone new? Did you start an important job, a new project? Were you away from home? Did something happen which changed your life or your ideas about life? Write one sentence each to describe the beginning, middle, and ending of that period.

For *My Life* think of your life as a continuum. Divide your life into three phases. You may choose school divisions, such as elementary, high school, college; you may divide your life into past, present, and future; or you may wish to divide your life into other periods. For each of the periods you choose, ask specific questions to bring that time into sharp focus. Where did you live? What was happening in your personal life? What was happening in the world during that time? Were things similar or different among all of these periods? Did your ideas or your ways of thinking or acting undergo changes? Did your ideas or actions remain the same? Did your friends and acquaintances change? Were your activities in each period different or similar? Did your life's goals undergo a transformation during any one of the three periods?

If you wish to reflect more deeply on the topics, use a separate sheet of paper for each of the three periods, and jot down your thoughts as they occur. Then use these random jottings to formulate the one-sentence descriptions to be placed on the blank chart. Save all the notes and jottings for use in a later chapter.

THE INDEPENDENT LEARNER'S NEED FOR REFLECTION

Looking at life and new learning situations from different perspectives grows in power and effect when you allow yourself time for planned, serious reflection. Reflection means turning back your thoughts, thinking again about anything, mentally going over experiences, events, or ideas. During reflection, you sort out and reorder ideas, see relationships between actions and their consequences, make comparisons, see contrasts and similarities. Reflective thinking helps you discover connections among incidents, personal experiences, and thoughts. Reflection is essential for significant learning. Although everyone reflects to some degree, few people plan for periods of reflection. Once you get into the habit of planned reflection you will use it for gaining knowledge in any area. It is particularly important to plan for a short period of reflection after each lecture or class you attend. Plan to reflect within a few hours of the class and reserve a few minutes for the exercise that follows.

REFLECTIONS AFTER CLASS

Before reviewing class notes or completing the assignment, write for two minutes to answer the questions below.

I. What was the most important thing I learned today?
   Why is it important?
   How might this knowledge affect me?
II. Was anything unclear about today's session?
   List all questions that occur to you.

While reviewing class notes

I. Look for beginnings, middles, and endings.
II. Mark in different colors the *this is what I am going to say* and *this is what I've said* statements.

After reviewing class notes and completing the assignment, write answers to the questions below.

I. Have all my questions (above) been answered?
   If not, place a check next to the questions to be asked in class at the next session.
II. How successful was today's work?
   How can I improve it?

As the habit of planned reflection becomes second nature, you will be analyzing your study habits to improve and refine your learning strategies. You will need a method for getting the most out of your textbooks and dealing with new and technical vocabularies. This chapter will deal briefly with these independent techniques so you can start to use them immediately.

As an independent learner, try each technique two or more times as described, then ask yourself the following questions about each: *Is this method working for me? What are its strengths? What are its weaknesses? How can I improve or adapt the method to fit my personal learning style?*

When you adapt a method to fit your style of learning, use it at least twice, then reflect again on the new approach. You may wish to change it once more before it feels most comfortable. On the other hand, the method as described may work for you as it has for others.

USING THE TEXTBOOK
CHECKLIST

The textbook is a specialized form, and because of its extended length and instructional nature, it is both complex and highly structured. Reading a textbook will be less stressful if you familiarize yourself with its contents from the start—at the beginning of a semester.

It is not unusual for students to spend hours with a dictionary, looking up technical terms, finding ten or more definitions for each one and trying to figure out which definition is appropriate to the context. Time-consuming searches for proper definitions are unnecessary if the textbook contains a *glossary*. The glossary of a text lists the single, most appropriate definition within the context of the material in the textbook.

Each component of a textbook is written to help you understand the contents; therefore, make it a practice to examine each of your texts carefully. Your examination will be thorough if you use the *Textbook Checklist* for each one of your course books. Begin with this book, now, and work your way through the book, writing down the items you encounter. When you use the *Textbook Checklist*, you will become aware of many of the book's time-saving features.

Textbook Checklist

Title _____

Author _____

Publisher _____

Publication date _____

Number of chapters _____

Number of pages _____

I. Check the items found in the textbook.

Foreword	_____	Appendix	_____
Introduction	_____	Index	_____
References	_____	Other	_____
Glossary	_____		

II. Read the Table of Contents.
Notice the major divisions of the book.
Leaf through the book. What is the format? Do the chapters follow a pattern?

What kind of pattern? Look at each chapter. *Write* one sentence describing the format or pattern of the chapters.

_____

_____

III. Check the subdivisions found in the chapters.

Introduction _____   Summaries _____

Subheadings _____   Questions _____

Activities   _____   Exercises _____

IV. Read the Foreword and the Introduction to the book.

BUILDING A BETTER VOCABULARY

New words are everywhere, increasing in number with each technological advance. It is essential to develop a method for understanding and adding new terms to your working vocabulary. Adding new words regularly to your personal vocabulary is another way of increasing your reading and writing skills. Try the approach that follows, then adapt it to your needs.

The moment you encounter a new word, take some action.

First, if you own the book, *underline* the new word. If it's not your book, *write* the new word down.

Second, *try to get the meaning from the context.* Read the sentence in which the word appears. Does the sentence give clues to the meaning of the word? Can you figure it out?

Third, look through your textbook (or textbook checklist) for a *glossary.* Glossaries define terms as they are used in the context of your book's subject.

Fourth, use a dictionary if no glossary exists. Try to find the definition that fits the context.

Fifth, make a permanent record of the word and its definition in your *Personal Vocabulary File.*

A Personal Vocabulary File

A personal vocabulary file serves three purposes. As a memory technique, it enables you to make associations with words you already know. As a resource, it expands your knowledge by adding to your supply of working words. As a study skill, it stores definitions for reviewing for examinations or when writing reports and papers.

Use a small looseleaf notebook or three-by-five cards or pads. Using the same size paper or cards for all your entries will make the system more efficient and easy to handle and the information will be readily available for quick reference.

1. On one side of a card, print or type the new word. If the word is difficult to pronounce, add the phonetic spelling from the dictionary.

Front of Card:

```
    WORD:   denotation


        PHONETIC SPELLING (as given in dictionary):


                    (dē' nō tā' shən)
```

2. On the other side of the card, write the definition that best fits the meaning of the sentence in which the word appears.

Back of Card:

```
        DEFINITION:   The explicit meaning of a word, as

    opposed to its connotation.

        PERSONAL MEMORY LINK:   Strong Association

                                Related Idea

                                Diagram or Drawing

                                Synonym and/or Antonym

        SENTENCE:
```

3. Add a personal memory link. Choose one or more of the following ways to link the meaning of the new word to something you already know: jot down the first strong association that occurs to you; write down a related idea; draw a diagram or picture; reflect on the new word and try to call up a *synonym*, a word that is similar in meaning, or an *antonym*, a word that is opposite in meaning.

4. Finally, write an original sentence using the new word, or copy the sentence in which it appeared (if you believe the sentence will be useful when you are studying for an examination in the subject).

Remember to use a new card or page for each word entered so the file can be organized in different ways, depending upon your needs. Generally, alphabetical filing is most efficient. However, when course vocabularies are new and technical, you may want to separate each subject's vocabulary, and then file the terms alphabetically under subject, or chapter-by-chapter. This will be especially helpful when you are studying for an exam. At the end of the term, you may wish to place all of the vocabulary cards in a single file, particularly in your major field of study, where you are likely to write extended reports and papers. After using the *Personal Vocabulary File* for a while, you will find the way that works best for you.

The act of adding words to a vocabulary file will increase your memory of them. Particularly helpful for recall is your choice of memory link, whether it is an association, synonym, sentence, or diagram. However, even memory joggers require periodic reviews to increase the chances of remembering over the long term. Another way of remembering new words is to use them in conversation or writing until they become integral parts of your working vocabulary. Moreover, if you expand the file to include new words from newspapers, magazines, and pleasure reading, your word knowledge will grow immensely.

SUMMARY

Independent learners take responsibility for their own learning by analyzing their study habits, learning styles, and experiences through the practice of planned reflection. They take it upon themselves to organize study groups, to look at things from different perspectives, to use a *Textbook Checklist*, to build better usable vocabularies, to monitor their own progress and learning.

Independent learners know that most uses of language in communication have three parts—beginnings, middles, and endings. When organized well, written materials have introductory sections, body sections, and concluding sections. Writers sometimes refer to the purposes of the three sections as *This is what I am going to say*; *This is where I say it*; *This is what I have said*. Readers and writers who understand the purposes of beginnings, middles, and endings and who are aware of similarities and differences among textual materials, tend to read with more understanding and to write with increased fluency.

Independent learners know there is usually more than one way to approach a task; they do not hesitate to originate learning strategies or to improve on those taught. By looking for connections and relationships among experiences and ideas and by constantly making comparisons and checking for differences, independent learners gather and retain new knowledge every day of their lives. They develop inquiring minds that constantly observe, question, and reflect. They fill notebooks with all sorts of notations and brief descriptions. Their shelves contain books marked with lines, arrows, highlights, notes, and questions. Their personal interests and hobbies are continuously growing and expanding. In short, independent learners look at all of life as an arena for learning.

INDEPENDENT ACTIVITIES

Reread the Introduction to this book and look for specific signs of a beginning, middle, and ending.

A. Draw a penciled line between the section you consider the beginning and the part you decide is the middle. Draw a line between the middle and the ending.
B. When you have divided the Introduction into three parts, pick out one sentence in the beginning section which says, in effect, "This is what I am going to say." Pick out one sentence in the ending section which says, "This is what I have said."

GROUP ACTIVITIES

Plan to share some of your ideas and notes about beginnings, middles, and endings with the class or a small group of friends. How does your description of a particular period compare with those of your friends or classmates? How are they the same? How are they different? Did most of your friends choose happy periods or good days? Were some of the descriptions sadder than others? Were some more dramatic or mysterious? Were others written matter-of-factly, as a newspaper report might be written?

There is no right or wrong way to complete this assignment. However, when you hear different students' styles of writing, you may wish to try new or different methods of expressing yourself on paper.

Discuss incidents in history, in the news, or on television, which can be summarized in three parts. Think about letters to friends, telephone conversations, TV commercials, or episodes in situation comedies. Can you find any uses of language for communication, written or spoken, which do *not* have beginnings, middles, or endings? Discuss these as well.

APPLICATION

During lectures: Listen for beginnings, middles, and endings in the instructor's presentation. Later, reread your lecture notes. Divide the notes into three parts, and underline *this is what I am going to say* and *this is what I have said* statements. Place a question mark next to notes that are unclear.

When taking exams: Look for beginnings, middles, and endings in essay questions. What does each part ask you to do? Reread the question after writing your answer. Did you attend to all of the sections? Does your answer have a beginning, middle, ending?

While studying: Spend a few minutes responding to "Reflections After Class." Review lecture notes to clear up portions in question.

As soon as possible: Complete a *Textbook Checklist* for each of your textbooks in other courses.

In other courses: Read all assignments using the "Building a Better Vocabulary" technique and start a personal vocabulary file.

two

The Flexible Reader

Are you wondering how you will ever get through all those textbooks you purchased at the bookstore? One student, carrying eight or nine books, remarked that he had not read nine books in his entire life. Another student said her textbooks *looked* different, far more complex than other books she had read. Are you having similar thoughts about your books?

Look at them for a moment. Flip through the pages of each one. Recall that without exception each book is made up of a number of smaller units—chapters. Think of each book as a package of individual chapters that you will be dealing with *one at a time*. By looking at your texts as a series of smaller, related units, you will feel less overwhelmed at the prospect of having to read all of them in one semester. As the author of this textbook, I, too, became overwhelmed at the prospect of writing the whole book. However, when I divided my material into smaller units, I was better able to handle the task.

Dealing with a long, complicated chapter may overwhelm you in much the same way, but there are two ways of handling long chapters. First, divide the chapter into smaller units, using the subdivisions created by the author. Choose a section you can read at one sitting and deal with that section as though it were a mini-chapter. Second, use more efficient strategies and variable rates of reading. In order to vary your rate of reading, you need to know your present reading rate. Rates of reading are calculated as the *number of words read per minute (wpm)*. How many words do you read in one minute? If you do not know your present rate of reading, prepare now to test yourself. You will need a stop watch or a clock with a sweep "second" hand. The idea is to determine how long it takes you to read Reading Passage Number One on page 126.

To determine your present reading rate, start reading when the second hand of the clock is on twelve, quickly jotting down the exact time. Read at your normal rate, the way you generally read a magazine or newspaper for enjoyment. After you have read the entire article, again jot down the time. Calculate the number of minutes you spent reading (eliminate odd seconds and round off the time to the nearest half minute). Use the convenient Personal Reading Rate Information chart to record this information which you will need for comparisons later. Then turn to the Words-Per-Minute Rate Chart on page 128 to find your reading rate for passage number one.

PERSONAL READING RATE INFORMATION

Date: _____

Starting time: _____

Stopping time: _____

Total number of minutes: _____

Number of words per minute: _____

When you have determined your reading rate, complete the Writing in Response to Reading exercise on page 24, then continue to read this chapter.

WHAT YOU CAN EXPECT FROM THIS CHAPTER

The purpose of this chapter is to help you become a flexible reader. You will learn how and when to adjust your general rate of reading. You will learn when to use fast, slow, or moderate rates of reading, depending upon the purpose and difficulty of the material. You will discover the benefits of *writing* in response to reading. You will plan a reading improvement program for yourself, from which you will learn to monitor your reading progress. You will practice the powerful skill of *skimming* at twice your general speed to preview central ideas in a passage.

WHAT IS A FLEXIBLE READER?

A flexible reader is one who can adjust his or her reading rate to the purposes and difficulties of the material to be read. Studies have shown that inflexible or rigid readers tend to use one rate only for all reading purposes. Rigid reading is simply a combination of ineffective reading habits and misinformation about the role the reading rate plays in understanding what is read.

CONTRASTS BETWEEN
FLEXIBLE AND RIGID READING

Two students researching different topics for the same term paper assignment are sitting at a table in the library. The table is stacked high with books. The first student reads quietly and continuously, rarely turning pages. Now and then, she glances at the large pile of books, then at her wristwatch, and sighs. The second student picks one book, glances at the table of contents and puts the book aside. She picks up another, checks the table of contents, flips to page 300, places a card in the page, and moves to another book. Which student is the flexible reader? Which student are you?

Students frequently complain of impatience with their slow reading rate and express the desire to take a course in speed reading. Somewhere in the past they heard that slow reading ensures better comprehension. Now, faced with volumes of new and technical subjects, they find slowness a handicap and are dismayed to learn that they do not understand enough material after the first reading of a chapter. In fact, some students admit they have to read a chapter three or four times.

The surprising truth is that reading too slowly can decrease comprehension and reading a chapter three or four times at the same slow pace may not necessarily increase understanding. On the other hand, speed reading may not be the solution. An efficient reader is not always a speed demon of the printed page. The efficient reader's technique is *flexibility*.

Before turning pages, efficient readers purposefully choose their pace. After a time, this decision-making process becomes second nature, as it will for you. As an efficient reader, you will not have to think consciously about your rate of reading. You may read a chapter more than once, but you will not read it the same way twice, nor will you look for the same kinds of information with each reading.

The efficient or flexible reader uses at least three different rates for reading—fast, moderate, and slow. Each rate is used for a different purpose, depending upon the sort of material being read and the degree of comprehension needed.

CLASSIFICATION OF RATES OF READING

Reading Rate	Purposes	Approximate Comprehension	wpm
Fast	*Skimming* for central ideas, thesis statement, conclusion, key information	50%	Varies—to 1000 wpm and higher
Moderate	*Moderate* Speed for general reading, close reading, details	70% or more	Varies—from 250 wpm up to 500 & higher
Slow	*Deliberate* Reading for difficult material, rereading for revision	80% to 90%	Varies—from 200-350 wpm and higher

HOW TO BECOME A FLEXIBLE READER

To become a flexible reader, continue to observe your reading habits, distractions, and pace. Try avoiding study areas where outside stimuli prevent you from concentrating. Read and apply the suggestions that follow to vary your reading rate and experiment with faster reading. *Write* in response to all of your reading assignments in other subjects. Study carefully the principles of comprehension which will be presented later in this chapter, and use them in your written responses to reading. Take seriously later discussions of the importance of daily reading practice and the personal program of pleasure reading. All are proven ways of becoming a flexible reader.

VARYING YOUR READING RATE

To vary your rate of reading, you need to know, as a basis of comparison, the general reading speed you calculated at the beginning of this chapter. The word *general* is used broadly to mean the pace you ordinarily use when *not* studying for an exam or when *not* skimming for a specific purpose. Comparisons will not be made between your rate and the so-called average rate of reading. What constitutes an average reading pace for you may be too slow or too fast for another student. The only question you must ask is, "Is the rate I am presently using appropriate for my immediate needs and purposes?"

Chances are your general reading pace feels natural most of the time. Depending on your past experiences and present needs, however, you may be dissatisfied with it. You may wish to speed up or slow down your general rate. If you have had little or no reason to accelerate your reading, you may very well be displeased with the pace you have acquired—and your present rate may indeed be too slow for your new academic needs. You are the only one who can determine what works best for you and you *can* change the outmoded reading habits that prevent you from attaining your goals.

The first step is to observe your present reading habits. Each time you prepare to read a passage or chapter, resolve to keep a close watch on what happens. Consider your level of concentration. Are you distracted easily? What kinds of outside stimuli tend to distract you? Are distractions more powerful when you read particular kinds of material or subjects? On the other hand, are there occasions when you are so thoroughly engrossed in reading that nothing short of a calamity can distract you? What subjects are you reading when you cannot be distracted? What are the factors that cause you to read more quickly or to slow down, to skip sentences or reread passages? Answer these questions by jotting down your observations. When most of the questions have been answered, begin to experiment with your reading speeds.

You can experiment with different speeds by reading a short passage, deliberately changing your rate of reading, and checking your understanding of the material with the Writing in Response to Reading method page 24. The experiment has two purposes. First, it will convince you that you have the power to change your rate of reading, and second, it will help you become more comfortable at a faster pace than your general rate. Begin by timing the short passage, Reading Passage Number Two on page 129, and plan to complete a timed reading at least once a day to ensure more flexibility.

EXPERIMENTING WITH FASTER READING

Set a timer for two minutes and plan to read Passage Two as quickly as you can. If you do not have a timer, use the sweep second hand of a clock and a tape recorder to make a two-minute timing tape or cassette which can be used over and over again.

TO MAKE A TWO-MINUTE TIMING TAPE

1. Turn on the tape and watch the clock.
2. When the second hand is on twelve, say, "Start" into the microphone. Keep watching the clock.
3. When the second hand reaches twelve again, after *two* minutes, say, "Stop."
4. Turn off the machine and rewind the tape.

You now have a two-minute timer which can be used for monitoring many reading exercises (or for cooking a two-minute egg).

When two minutes pass, count the number of words you have read, *then divide the number by two*. This is your actual reading rate for the passage. To check your understanding, complete the Writing in Response to Reading exercise (below) as you did for the first passage.

Now compare your new, faster rate with the general rate you computed at the beginning of this chapter. What is the difference? How did it feel to read faster than your general rate? Were you comfortable or did you experience discomfort? What happened to your level of understanding when you accelerated reading speed? Compare your written "responses" to the passages. Did you remember more details when you read quickly, or was your comprehension better at your general rate?

Do not be surprised if your comprehension decreases significantly at the faster rate; this is quite normal. As you continue to do more of the two-minute timed readings, your faster rate will feel more comfortable and your level of comprehension will increase.

Do not be discouraged if your faster rate of reading is the same as or close to your general pace. You may need to practice faster reading a number of times, increasing your speed gradually until you feel comfortable with it. Changing old, familiar habits into new ones rarely happens over night. With reading, as with any other skill, practice is essential. Most important, you will have at your disposal two rates of reading from which to choose, and you will be well on your way to becoming a flexible reader.

WRITING IN RESPONSE TO READING

The practice of writing in response to reading is essential to increasing your comprehension of a passage. When you complete the Writing in Response to Reading exercise, you are in effect answering the question "What is the passage about?" *What is the passage about?* is a *general* question, one which gives little information as to *how* one would go about answering it. Questions one, three, and four of Writing in Response to Reading are, on the other hand, more *specific*, clearly telling you what to look for when answering the question "What is the passage about?" In short, the practice of responding to reading by writing provides the direction you need for increasing your comprehension.

WRITING IN RESPONSE TO READING

Upon completing the reading of a passage, do the following exercise:

1. Quickly write your impression of the author's main points or central ideas. Continue writing freely for two minutes, or as long as ideas continue to occur.
2. Write a summary of your response to item one (above) in a single sentence.
3. Write one sentence or more from the passage which tells what the selection is about: *This is what I'm going to say.*
4. Write one sentence or more from the passage which reveals the conclusion: *This is what I have said.*
5. List the ways in which the ideas expressed in the passage relate (or do not relate) to you, your life, your ideas.

UNDERSTANDING YOUR LEVELS OF COMPREHENSION

The whole concept of how one gets meaning from the printed word is as complex as the study of the mind itself. Yet even minimal knowledge of different levels of comprehension can increase your understanding of a passage. For now, it is sufficient for you to know what these levels are. Later in this text, you will see how the levels apply to reading/writing competencies. Three levels will be discussed briefly—the literal level, the inferential level, and the critical level.

Literal Comprehension

The Literal Level of Comprehension is the first one learned in school. In literal understanding, the reader recognizes and recalls *facts*. The word *literal* comes from the Latin word *litera* which means *letter*; therefore, a *literal translation* is one that is performed "to the letter" or without changes. Literal questions ask you to recall or identify. They frequently ask Who? What? When? Where? Literal comprehension is the first taught because it is the basis for the other levels of understanding. Without the facts, a reader would have trouble with the inferential and critical levels.

Inferential Comprehension

The Inferential Level of Comprehension requires an understanding of relationships among ideas and concepts. First, the reader distinguishes between general and specific ideas. In other words, what is the author's central thought? And what are the specific details offered to support that central thought? Second, the reader must be able to draw conclusions from the written facts. Inferential comprehension is sometimes referred to as "reading between the lines."

Reading between the lines is something you do every day. For example, if you read a newspaper story about a fire that says, "traces of kerosene and match sticks were found in the burnt rubble," what might you conclude? There are a number of conclusions you might draw: (a) either the matches or the kerosene caused the fire; (b) someone either left or brought the incendiary materials to the scene; (c) the fire had a suspicious origin. Notice that the reporter or writer presents the facts, but the facts *imply* something more. The implications, in turn, cause the reader to *infer* that there is something more to the story. Finally, inferential comprehension enables a reader to get deeper meaning from the printed word, to literally "read between the lines," and to answer the question *Why?*.

Critical Comprehension

The Critical Level of Comprehension is the level at which the reader questions, evaluates, and judges the material. The reader may weigh or compare the writer's ideas with his or her own ideas, or may use other known values as yardsticks by which to measure what the writer says. The reader may ask general questions of the text such as, Is it fact or opinion? Are the conclusions valid? Is the reasoning logical? The critical reader is a questioning reader who asks, "How is this so? Where is the proof? Why am I to believe what is said?" Critical comprehension, as well as inferential and literal comprehension, must be seen as extensions of *thinking*. Levels of thinking, in turn, can develop and expand through extensive reading, questioning, reflecting, and expressing thoughts in writing.

PLANNING YOUR PERSONAL
READING PROGRAM:
THE READING LOG

One way of getting yourself to read more is to choose a book that is so intriguing you cannot put it down. What book have you always wanted to read but never gotten around to? *Roots? The Godfather? Ordinary People?* Think for a moment, and decide which book you will choose for your personal reading program.

The book you choose to read does not have to be a classic or literary masterpiece, but it must be a story that grabs you from the start, from the first few pages. If it doesn't hold your interest, try another one. Have you always wanted to read a James Bond saga, a Harlequin romance, or an Agatha Christie mystery? Now is the time to do it.

Check the paperback rack in the bookstore. Is there a title which flags your attention? What about the best seller list? Is there something a friend recommended that you made a mental note to buy or to borrow from the library? Have you seen a great movie recently that is also in book form? Have you ever read *Gone With the Wind, Harold and Maude, Kramer Versus Kramer*? Have you ever read a film script? Many film scripts are published in paperback form. Have you ever read a play? Now is the time to pick the book you have always wanted to read but thought you didn't have time for. *This is going to be an assignment you'll thoroughly enjoy.*

THE READING LOG

The *Reading Log* is part of the daily personal reading program and will take, at most, a half hour of your time. You will need a book to read and a notebook in which to log your daily reading. There is one restriction only on the book you choose; it cannot be related to school work, to any course assignment, or to any job project. You will have your fill of work-related reading; this assignment must be *pure pleasure.*

To complete the Reading Log assignment, read from your book each day for twenty minutes only and respond in one sentence to each twenty-minute reading. In your Reading Log, include the following information for each reading session:

Date: _____

Starting time: _____

Stopping time: _____

Number of pages read (e.g., pp. 1-10): _____

Write one sentence in response to the reading: _____

_____

_____

There are a number of ways to accomplish the one-sentence response to the daily reading.

1. You may summarize what you have read.
2. You may react to the text.
3. You may comment on your feelings after reading.
4. You may copy a particular sentence (for any reason) from the text.
5. You may choose another way of responding.

If the Reading Log assignment sounds weird or unusual to you, let me tell you what you can expect from twenty minutes of reading and the writing of a one-sentence response. First, research shows that the simple practice of reading is one of the most powerful ways of gaining skill in comprehension and of becoming a more flexible reader. The exercise of reading is not altogether different from other forms of exercise. At first you may experience stiffness and some mild discomfort, but eventually, the action becomes second nature, and you may wonder why you stayed away from the activity for so long.

Second, the Reading Log will enable you to clearly monitor your reading rate and habits. You may discover that you can read ten pages of a chapter in twenty minutes at one time, yet complete only five pages at another sitting. Why does this happen? You will discover that certain times are better than others for reading. You will discover that although reading fiction involves very different skills than those involved in reading textbooks and other kinds of expository writing, the act of reading fiction can enhance your understanding of nonfiction. On the other hand, although fiction and nonfiction differ in content, style, tone, and purpose, both have beginnings, middles, and endings. Your written reactions to various passages will develop and refine your awareness of these differences. Responding in writing to reading will pique your interest in certain subjects, particular authors, and various styles of writing—all of which can enhance your growth as a more critical reader.

Third, through the Reading Log you will encounter subjects, people, and worlds you never knew existed. Books and ideas will influence and develop your personal values. Changing values and ideas can change your life and can help you to know yourself and others in a more insightful way. Decide now to give yourself the *gift* of reading for pure pleasure. You deserve it.

SUMMARY

Flexibility in reading is a sign of an efficient reader. Flexibility is achieved through an awareness of reading rate, practicing different speeds, and understanding levels of comprehension. Good readers vary their reading speeds according to particular purposes of reading and the nature of the text. One way of becoming a flexible reader is to read for pure pleasure every day.

INDEPENDENT ACTIVITIES

I. *Read* only the headings in this chapter.

Reflect on the headings, and divide them into two classifications: (1) general information; and (2) specific learning strategies. List the headings on a sheet of paper in two columns:

General	Specific

Write a one-sentence summary (without looking back to reread sections) for each heading in the *Specific* column. The purpose of each sentence is to explain to another person how the strategy works.

Reread the section under each heading to see if your sentence explains clearly the strategy taught. Revise all sentences that are not clear.

Write your own definition to explain the differences between *general* and *specific*. Either define the terms in your own words, or describe them as they apply to the headings in this chapter. In other words, why did you place some headings in the *General* column and others in the *Specific?*

II. *Reread* Chapter One while changing your reading rate every few paragraphs from fast to slow to moderate. Jot down what happens at each speed. Which speed feels most comfortable? Which is uncomfortable? At which rate of reading is your understanding of the text most complete?

Read your textbook assignments in the same way, experimenting until you find the best pace for the kind of material you are reading. Do you find you can read a biology text faster than an algebra book? Do you read essays more quickly than biology? At what rate do you read for pleasure?

Reflect for a few minutes each time you begin reading, and jot down answers to the following questions:

Why am I reading this particular piece?
What do I want to know?
What do I already know about the subject?
What is the best way to read this material?

Write for ten minutes about your planned personal reading program. Describe the kinds of books, movies, or stories that have intrigued you in the past. Are there certain subjects, settings, or authors that hold your interest most? Which subjects hold least interest for you? What do you expect from a good book? What generalizations can you make about your personal reading interests, habits, and preferences? What do you expect from your planned reading program?

III. *Read* the selections "Why Do We Sleep" and "Every 90 Minutes, A Brainstorm" (pages 141 and 142 in the Appendix).

Reflect on each selection, then complete the Writing in Response to Reading exercise (page 24) for each one.

Write for a few minutes (after completing the exercises) about the way *Writing in Response to Reading* is working for you. Might the exercise work better if you could adapt it to your particular needs? Would adding another question increase its usefulness? Perhaps the addition of subject or chapter-specific questions would make it even more useful.

Plan to discuss your ideas about the Writing in Response to Reading exercise in class or in a small group.

GROUP ACTIVITIES

I. *Share* the one-sentence summaries from Independent Activity I in class or with a group of friends. Read the sentence aloud. Could another person *use* the specific learning strategy after hearing your sentence? Discuss the responses, and listen to others' sentences. What conclusions or generalizations can you draw about explaining a process or strategy to another person?

Discuss your definition or explanation of the terms "general" and "specific." Listen to others' definitions. What conclusions can you draw from your own and other students' explanations of the terms? In the light of the group discussion, can you improve or change your definition of general versus specific?

II. *Share* your personal reading program ideas (Independent Activity II) in class or with a small group of friends. Listen to the titles others have chosen to read. Jot down titles or authors that sound interesting; you may want to read them at another time. Share with the group your ten-minute writing about reading.

Discuss your experiment in different rates of reading. Listen to the problems or successes expressed by others in class. You can learn a great deal from one another. Try some of the strategies others have tried. This is one way of discovering which methods work best for you.

Compare your Writing in Response to Reading with other students' responses. Does your group agree or disagree about the passage's central ideas? When the group disagrees, reread aloud parts of the passage for confirmation and further discussion. What conclusions or generalizations can you draw from hearing other students' responses to the reading?

APPLICATION

In other courses: Keep a reading log for subjects that are complex or troublesome. Reserve a section in the back of the subject notebook for the log. Respond in writing to each chapter you read. Clock your reading rate and adjust it for more efficiency. Record questions that occur as you read, questions which may be answered in class by the instructor or through further reading. Use the one-sentence response to summarize short sections of text. Through the log's running commentary on your progress in the course, you will recognize your areas of strength as well as areas in which you may need further work or development.

During lectures: While taking notes, place question marks near passages that are not immediately clear. Turn those notes into questions for which you must locate answers.

While studying: Instead of reading a chapter from start to finish, read shorter segments. Respond to each short segment by writing one-sentence summaries as soon as you complete each section. To test your understanding of the section, reread it, checking the facts against your responses. Rest your eyes between sections, giving yourself time to reflect on what you have read and written. If you continue to have difficulty reading or understanding a text, take your reading log in hand and initiate a conference with your instructor.

When taking examinations: Allow time for rereading questions and for checking your answers against each question. Rest your eyes and mind between questions.

three

The Fluent Writer

PREPARATION FOR
CHAPTER THREE

How do you feel about writing? Do you like to write? Do you dislike it? How do you react when faced with a writing assignment and a blank sheet of paper? Do words flow easily and freely, or is writing sometimes a painfully slow process?

Before reading this chapter, reflect for a while on the questions posed in the preceding paragraph, then write about writing. Simply jot down your thoughts as they occur. Write for a full ten minutes without stopping. As you focus on your feelings about writing, try to include answers to the following questions as well: *Why* do you feel as you do about writing? *Where* did the feelings begin—at home, in school, elsewhere? *When* did you first become aware of these feelings about writing? *What* caused them? As a result, *how* do you see yourself as a writer?

While you are writing, do not be concerned with spelling, grammar, or handwriting. The goal of this ten-minute exercise is to explore your personal attitudes about and experiences with writing. Finally, after writing for ten minutes, read everything you wrote. Skip two or three spaces on the paper and answer these questions: What is the meaning of your experience? In other words, what conclusion or generalization can you draw from your own words? Write your conclusion or generalization in one sentence. Then, put the ten-minute writing aside and continue reading this chapter.

WHAT YOU CAN EXPECT
FROM THIS CHAPTER

The purpose of this chapter is to help you become a fluent writer. You will learn that writing is both a process and a craft and that once you understand the process, the craft can be developed more readily. You will learn that different modes of writing are required for different purposes. You will use writing as a tool for learning and as a method of discovery—to find out what it is that you really want to say. You will discover the value and enjoy the benefits of keeping different kinds of journals and logs. You will plan your personal writing program. Later on, you will learn to evaluate your writing progress. The increased practice in writing will lead to a better understanding of techniques for writing term papers, taking essay examinations, and comprehending other writers' ideas.

WHAT IS A FLUENT WRITER?

A fluent writer is one who is able to write at will most of the time. Fluent writers tend to *think on paper*, writing whatever comes to mind, frequently learning and discovering what they think *only* when the ideas have moved from their minds, through their pens, to the paper. They have learned that writing is an ongoing process of discovery, reflection, and change. They use writing as a tool for learning, a method of communication, and a way of planning projects and developing ideas.

Most important, fluent writers clearly expect their first writing efforts or first drafts to be meandering, repetitious, fragmented, and error-laden collections of ideas. They permit random thoughts to tumble from their minds because they realize the importance of catching fleeting thoughts quickly, before they become lost or forgotten. Fluent writers are not fearful of making mistakes, misspellings, or incorrect grammar. They know they can change, shape, and polish their prose at another time. Fluent writers are not naïve enough to believe that writing is an easy task, but they are the first to admit that the constant use of writing for varied reasons makes it easier to get started, keep going, and to reread, reflect, and rewrite. In other words, fluent writers have learned to unblock the flow of words.

CONTRASTS BETWEEN FLUENT
AND BLOCKED WRITING

Two students assigned the same writing project are sitting at a table in a quiet corner of the library. The first student writes on a yellow, ruled pad with a ball point pen. Now and then he pauses, looks away, then continues writing. Sometimes he crosses out words or phrases, inserting others to replace them. Once in a while he rereads what he has written. When a friend enters, calls to him, and waves, he does not notice. The second student, biting the eraser at the end of his pencil, has decorated his yellow, ruled pad with airplanes which he has drawn with great artistic detail. He is distracted by everyone entering the library and waves to all who pass by. Do you recognize yourself in either of the students?

If you are like most students, you probably have experienced moments of fluency as well as periods of blocked writing. Even professional writers admit that their degree of fluency fluctuates. Most have found, however, that the practice of writing *on command* is the only way to prevent excessive blocking. Many inexperienced or unpracticed student writers are blocked because they believe they must know what they think *before* putting words on paper. They may stare endlessly at a blank page waiting for the perfect opening sentence to flow full-blown from pen or typewriter. In contrast, more practiced writers realize that the *act* of writing is the *key* to unblocking the flow of words. Indeed, the more practiced students, like professional writers, have discovered that writing can be used in a number of different ways.

Classification of Ways
of Writing

Through the exercises in this book, you will be practicing a great deal of writing; however, your approaches to the actual writing may vary, depending upon your purposes. The text will concentrate on three modes of writing: First, *Free Writing* for generating new ideas and planning a paper or report; Second, *Focused Writing* for arranging related central and supporting ideas in logical order; Third, *Formal Writing* for organizing groups of ideas or purposeful paragraphs into a coherent whole (essay or report).

Although the method used in this text takes you through a process *step by step* you may discover that your way of putting ideas on paper will vary from the order described. Writing is not a process that moves in a straight line, one step following another. Chances are, your movements will be varied, turning and winding in different directions as you move through each phase. During the process you will backtrack to reread or rewrite, or move forward to add or expand ideas. You will pause to cross out or change words. Each paper you write, in fact, may take you through the writing process in a new way.

HOW TO BECOME A FLUENT WRITER

To become a fluent writer, make the decision now to do most of your thinking, planning, and problem solving on paper. With continuous practice, the act of writing becomes comfortable and rewriting becomes easier. Professional writers claim that daily writing is the only road to both fluency and mastery of the craft.

You will know you are on the road to mastery when, after a satisfying prewriting phase of research, reflection, and free writing, your first draft seems to write itself. When this happens you can be sure you have done something right. Chances are, after researching and free writing on the topic, you allowed your ideas to incubate or to grow in the back of your mind while you were occupied with other matters. When this occurs, the subconscious mind usually is given the credit. Writers know that the subconscious plays a primary role in their work. Furthermore, some have learned to work with the subconscious, giving it a chance to develop stored ideas.

Haven't you had the experience of working on a difficult problem to the point of exhaustion, finally giving up on it, and then, while you were relaxing or busy doing something else totally unrelated to the problem, suddenly the solution came to you? Some call the phenomenon a flash of insight. Others call it a moment of inspiration or the work of the subconscious. Writers refer to it as the influence of the *muse*.

In classical mythology, muses were goddesses of the arts who had the power to inspire poets and writers. In many ways each artist creates a muse by the way he or she works. If you get into the habit of working on your writing assignments early, taking time each day to gather materials and to jot down ideas, allowing yourself time and space to get a sense of the beginning, middle, and ending of your project, your muse will get in touch with you. You will recognize the muse when, indeed, a first draft seems to write itself. When this happens you will know it is because you have a clear idea of the shape and content of your project and you have an understanding of your own writing processes.

UNDERSTANDING THE WRITING PROCESS

Many researchers and writers agree that writing is a three-stage process that logically includes the actions a writer takes *before, during,* and *after* the actual writing of a first draft. The *before* stage is called *prewriting*; the *after* stage is called *rewriting*.

Prewriting, the first stage, includes everything a writer does to prepare for writing a first draft. Depending on the nature of the writing task, writers in the first stage search for ideas by gathering materials, reading source books, listening, thinking, and jotting down notes and random thoughts. Jotting down random thoughts or *Free Writing* is part of the prewriting stage because it is a way of gathering facts and stored ideas from the mind. Writing quickly, as thoughts occur, without regard for correct spelling, grammar, or sentence structure, stimulates the free flow of words. Free writing, therefore, is a way of sifting through accumulations of past experiences, stored knowledge, and immediate thoughts.

Free writing during the prewriting stage is a way of solving problems or answering questions. Some of your first questions may include: What is my purpose in writing? Who is my reader, my audience? What do I really want to say? What is the clearest way of saying it?

Writing, the second stage, is the actual time spent putting words on paper *after some sort of decision has been made about the subject and the writing approach.* If enough time has been spent in free writing, the first draft may be quite focused. The second stage is a good time to see that you are sticking to your subject and supporting statements with facts or examples. During this stage, a writer also may jot down unrelated ideas to be used later. He or she may read or reread source materials, sit and think, or get up and take a walk. The writer may pause in the writing, cross out words, tear up papers, rewrite certain portions, and cross out some more. Some writers experience discouragement, fatigue, or a mixture of elation and gloom during this production stage. Some writers eat a lot.

Rewriting, the third stage, is a *craft* phase, and at the same time, a creating phase. It consists of critically rereading a completed or partially completed draft with the idea of rewriting, reformulating, and reordering information. During this stage, the writer tries to look at the work as an editor or teacher would. Being objective about one's own writing will take some practice, but it can be done. Rewriting can be the most exciting stage of writing because much deep thought has preceded it, and new combinations of ideas are constantly forthcoming.

MANAGING TIME FOR AN ASSIGNMENT

The quality of a report or paper often depends upon the way you have managed the time given for the assignment. Sitting at a typewriter, reading the assignment for the first time on the day it is due is one way of guaranteeing a poor product and perhaps a less than average grade. Why? Because writing takes time and thought and space. An independent learner uses every resource at hand when dealing with a writing assignment. Follow the day-by-day approach and watch the quality of your assignments improve.

Within a day of receiving the assignment, preread your assignment carefully. Free write for a few minutes, jotting down notes, ideas, and first thoughts about how you will deal with the assignment. First thoughts may include a sequence of steps you may have to take even before beginning the actual work, particularly if outside research is needed. When you run out of ideas, put the assignment aside.

The following day, reread your original notes and free write again, adding thoughts and ideas as they occur. When ideas run dry, put the assignment aside. If outside research is required, jot down the sources you will need to locate, and carry the list of sources with you.

On each succeeding day, before you actually begin to write a first draft, reread and add new ideas and material to your notes. When you are in the library or bookstore, skim the shelves for information related to your topic. Keep pen and pad handy at all times, even in front of the television set, to jot down ideas that may occur spontaneously.

Set up a file folder or large envelope, clearly labeled, in which all notes and source materials for the project will be stored. Do this, in fact, for each project or extended assignment in all of your courses, and keep the folders or envelopes accessible. By doing this, you keep the kernel of an idea uppermost in your mind, yet you also allow it to sink into the subconscious and simmer while you attend to unrelated matters. Then when you begin to write the first draft of your essay or report, you already will have given the topic a great deal of thought, and a surprisingly large number of new ideas will continue to filter into your conscious mind when you least expect them.

The day-by-day approach to writing will change and develop as you grow in your reading and writing competencies. At first, much of your free writing may be in the form of such questions as, What do I want to write about? What do I want to say? Why have I chosen this topic? If the topic was an assigned one, Would I have chosen a similar topic? How can I slant the topic more toward my personal interests? Explore all the questions that come up, then answer them as though you were having a conversation with another person. The more words you put on paper, the more material you have to work with, to reorder, reorganize, or discard. Remember, to be effective, free writing should be *free*. Do not worry about form or structure or correctness—just get the thoughts on paper.

Free writing can go on forever, but deadlines and assignment due dates arrive quickly. Never leave yourself short, with only a day or so for writing a draft, rewriting, and typing. Plan to allow yourself enough time to write the first draft and to let it cool at least overnight. Allow yourself time for at least one careful rewrite and enough time for rereading and editing two or three times.

You might like to try this method: Immediately upon receiving an assignment, divide the time remaining among prewriting, writing, and rewriting. In this way, you will not feel rushed at the end, and chances are you will produce a better paper. Another way of managing time is to allow half the time for prewriting and the other half for writing and rewriting. You will soon find the appropriate time management techniques that work best for you, although you may also find that each assignment has its own time demands.

One word of caution: do not let prewriting take up too long a period. If you are running short of time, write the first draft on the day you had planned, even if it means more free writing and exploring *after* the draft is written.

The day-by-day method of writing is used by many professional writers, who in fact have three or four writing projects going at the same time. The method will give momentum to your work and your creative processes. When you have used the technique for a while, writer's block will not trouble you because you will be a fluent writer.

EVALUATING YOUR OWN WORK

In college, as in life, writers always have deadlines to meet. It is not unusual, therefore, as you pull the last page from your typewriter, to suddenly think of an entirely different approach that would make your paper much stronger. But of course it *is* too late, for the class in which the paper is due meets in ten minutes. When this happens you may feel a momentary pang of regret, but soon regret turns to relief because the paper is finished and you do not have to think about it anymore. But what happens to that flash of insight that would improve the paper significantly? It's gone. You can be sure of that. Would it not be better to record that bit of information for future use, perhaps for the next paper you will write? Wouldn't that be another way of becoming a better writer and independent learner?

You *can* record those valuable second thoughts by taking a few moments to evaluate your paper before you turn it in. Indeed, self-evaluation may produce insights unattainable in other ways. To conduct a self-evaluation for each paper or report you write, respond to each of the seven items on the *Self-Evaluation* which follows this paragraph. When the instructor returns the paper to you, compare his or her comments with your own. Better yet, offer to submit a *Self-Evaluation* with each of your papers. Both you and the instructor will learn more about your writing processes—another bit of knowledge that will aid in your growth as an independent learner.

SELF-EVALUATION*

In self-evaluation, you will be commenting on your own writing and establishing your own goals for improvement.

1. How much time did you spend on this paper?
2. What did you try to improve on this paper? How successful were you? If you have questions about what you were trying to do, what are they?
3. What are the strengths of your paper? Place a check mark beside those passages you feel are very good.
4. What are the weaknesses, if any, of your paper? Place an *X* beside passages you would like corrected or revised. Place an *X* over any punctuation, spelling, usage, etc., where you need help or clarification.
5. What *one thing* will you do to improve your next piece of writing?
6. What would you do *differently* on this paper if you had more time?
7. Write a one-sentence summary of this self-evaluation.

PREPARING
A PROFESSIONAL-LOOKING
PAPER

If your instructor does not specify a particular format for written reports and papers, this one can be used for most subjects and courses.

1. Use plain white, unruled paper.
2. Type everything double-spaced. (Also, check a style manual for extended quotations and footnote formats.)

---

*Items 1-5 (Self-Evaluation) adapted from M.H. Beaven, "Individualized Goal Setting, Self-Evaluation, and Peer Evaluation," in *Evaluating Writing,* by C.R. Cooper, and L. Odell (Urbana, Illinois: National Council of Teachers of English, 1977), p. 143.

3. Type your name, class, and date on three separate lines in the upper left-hand corner of the first page.

4. Begin the typing halfway down the first page with your title in capital letters.

5. Type your last name or a word from the title in the uppermost left-hand corner of every page except the first.

6. Type the page number in the upper right-hand corner of every page except the first.

7. Leave generous 1½ inch margins on all sides.

8. Make corrections carefully by drawing one line through a word and inserting the correction above it. If you omit a letter or word, use a *caret* (an upside down v) to point it out and print the ommission neatly above it.

9. If there is a distracting number of corrections on a page, retype the entire page.

10. If you choose to use a cover page, place your name, class, and date at the upper left-hand corner, and the title in capital letters in the center of the page. Begin page one, halfway down, but eliminate the title if you use a cover page.

PLANNING YOUR PERSONAL WRITING PROGRAM: THE DAILY JOURNAL

Scientists and artists always have kept journals, and today more business people, teachers, and students are turning to journal keeping as their lives become increasingly complex with demands on their personal time multiplying and growing. Journals are kept for a number of reasons: to record and examine daily events and feelings, to follow a special project or experiment to completion, to monitor progress, to fill a specific need, such as the changing of a habit, to solve problems, or to reflect. For many students, a ten-minute journal entry each day provides just enough extra writing practice to assure a growing facility with written language and an increasing confidence with the act of writing.

Students who are newcomers to journal keeping frequently begin with straightforward diary-like entries such as, *I got up, ate breakfast, fed the cat, and went out.* But before long the dullness of such entries moves them to write on a deeper level. Instead of logging actions, they analyze them; instead of stating names of places visited, they describe the places, the weather, and people. Gradually, writing flows more freely, ideas form quickly, and time devoted to the journal grows precious, much like an oasis on a long stretch of desert.

Begin by choosing a special notebook for your journal and write your first entry today. (Some writers reserve a favorite writing instrument for journal entries.) Write whatever comes to mind and continue writing for ten minutes. If you cannot think of anything to write, write "I cannot think of anything to write." Then ask yourself, in writing, "Why can't I think of anything to write?" and list possible reasons. If you continue to feel blocked, pick a word, and write all the ideas that come to mind that are associated with the word. Do not give up. Before long words will flow, and you may not want to stop writing even at the end of ten minutes.

Journal writing has a long and enduring history, and when you become a daily journal keeper, you can expect good things to happen. First, your writing will improve. Writers know that daily writing enhances fluency and skill. Second, you will avoid writer's block. Writing daily can prevent your staring for long periods of time at a blank sheet of paper. Third, you will think more clearly. The practice of writing helps to organize thoughts. By reflecting on ideas and events, you discover new insights about yourself and others. Fourth, your reading will improve. Recent research has shown that students who wrote for only ten minutes a day, within the span of one semester, improved significantly in reading comprehension. In addition to enabling you to follow an idea or an experience for an extended period, your journal can become a fruitful source of ideas for writing projects and assignments. Most important, through journal writing you will become a fluent writer.

In summary, fluency in writing is the sign of a practicing writer. Fluency can be achieved by understanding writing as a process and by efficiently managing assignment time. Fluent writers tend to think on paper, do some writing every day, and use writing as a tool for learning.

INDEPENDENT ACTIVITIES

Reread the section in Chapter Three "Understanding the Writing Process." For each of the three phases (prewriting, writing, rewriting) write one summary sentence to describe the method or approach you have used in the past. Write a second summary sentence to describe one new method or approach that you will try for your next writing assignment.

Read the two summary sentences for each phase, then write one more sentence that summarizes the first two.

Reflect for a few minutes on your previous writing experiences in school, in business, and in your personal life. How were you taught to write? How much writing did you do? What kinds of writing were required?

Write for ten minutes about the way you feel at this moment about the daily journal assignment. Have you practiced journal writing before? Are there certain past events in your life that you have recorded or wish you had recorded? Are there, on the other hand, certain ideas or feelings that you would not want to put in writing? What are your immediate plans for using the daily journal? Will you attempt to solve a problem, monitor your progress in a particular area, or will you use the daily log for recording momentary thoughts? What generalizations or conclusions can you make about your present attitude toward the daily journal assignment?

GROUP ACTIVITIES

Share with the class or a small group of friends a selected entry from your writing about the daily journal assignment.

Listen to the responses of others. Jot down ideas for other uses of the journal that may not have occurred to you before the discussion.

Discuss with other students your feelings about writing.

Listen to other students' responses. Is there general agreement or disagreement among your group about feelings toward writing? What conclusions can you draw from the group discussion?

Talk about your experiences with the three phases of the writing process.

Share with the group your problems, questions, successes.

Listen to others' experiences. You can learn a great deal about writing from listening to others talk about their methods; try some of the strategies others have used. This is one way of discovering the methods that work best for you.

What conclusions or generalizations can you draw from your own and other students' experiences with writing?

APPLICATION

In other courses: Expand your journal to other subjects. Reserve a section in the back of the subject notebook where you can record feelings about your progress or problems with the course. The subject journal is one way of organizing random ideas and notes that may not fit into a *class notes* category or into your reading log section. It is a way of accumulating data and developing ideas, a way of holding on to pertinent thoughts and questions. In addition, your journal notes will come in handy when you confer with your course instructor.

During lectures: Write down comments and questions as they occur during a lecture; later, if you wish to develop them further, transfer them to your journal.

While studying: If ideas for assignments, reports, or projects occur to you, write them down quickly before you forget them—this is how professional writers hold on to and develop ideas.

Before handing in assignments: Complete a "Self-Evaluation."

Prepare all assignments in a professional way: Make use of the guidelines presented in Preparing a Professional-Looking Paper on page 39.

four

Pre-Reading/Writing: Literal Understanding

PREPARATION FOR CHAPTER FOUR

You are well-prepared for this chapter if you have put into practice the principles described in Chapters One through Three. Are you looking for beginnings, middles, and endings? Are you monitoring your reading habits and experimenting with different speeds? Have you chosen a book to read for pure pleasure, and are you logging your daily reading? Are you writing in a journal ten minutes a day? Are you using the journal technique in other subjects? Are you building your working vocabulary, using the personal vocabulary file method? Are you managing your time more efficiently by pacing each assignment? If your answers to these questions are affirmative, you are ready for Chapter Four. If, however, you have not completed an earlier chapter, or if you have not worked at least once with each strategy taught, please go back, catch up, then continue to read this chapter.

WHAT YOU CAN EXPECT
FROM THIS CHAPTER

The first phase of the reading/writing process is a preparation stage. During this phase, you as reader/writer, pose questions and establish purposes to get factual meaning from the text and to generate factual or literal ideas for an original essay. In so practicing *literal understanding*, you prepare yourself for the second stage, which involves a closer inspection of details. Students who skip over the preliminary phase and plunge into a task or a text with neither preparation nor purpose frequently get bogged down with details, lose direction and, as a result, spend an excessive amount of time rereading and rewriting (the third phase of the process).

Chapter Four introduces *skimming and free writing*, a powerful method for getting the gist of an author's work quickly and developing a topic for an original essay. This chapter takes you through the procedure step by step, then, to reinforce your learning of the concept, immediately offers opportunities to practice the skill. However, authentic learning of the technique takes place when you apply it to assignments in other subjects and when you adapt the method to fit your academic needs and personal learning style.

The intent of the skimming and free writing method is not to change your way of gaining knowledge or conform your style of learning to that of others'. Instead, it is offered because it works, and it works *quickly* to get you through reading and writing assignments with understanding and fluency. When the techniques taught here are assimilated into your mode of learning, they may be unrecognizable, but they will still contain the essential elements of the method. You, as a learning person, will choose, change, or reject everything you are taught, but you cannot make authentic choices, changes, or rejections until you have experienced the techniques in question. Skimming and free writing must be experienced to be appreciated.

SKIMMING AND FREE WRITING

The verb *skim* means to move over any surface quickly. A seagull skims the ocean for food; a motorized skimmer removes debris from the water's surface; cream that rises to the top of milk is skimmed off to leave *skim* milk.

Skimming is a technique for capturing the central ideas of a chapter, book, or essay without reading every word. It is a way of getting the gist of a text in a short time. Skimming is handy in the library for surveying a large number of books to determine which to use for a research project. It is also a way of prereading a chapter or essay to increase understanding of concepts and to note the organization of the piece.

Free Writing is a way of skimming ideas from the "top of the mind." It is a technique for generating central ideas for an original essay or term paper before "digging deeper" to write in detail. It is a way of outlining in a short time. Free writing is useful in exploring new ideas or for culling information from past experience. It is also a way of generating central ideas from a body of accumulated research.

Skimming and free writing are complementary processes. Skimming extracts, or takes out, central ideas from an author's text; free writing generates or brings out central thoughts from an author's mind.

THE POWER OF SKIMMING

The power of skimming can be demonstrated by *reading* a photograph in one glance. Turn to page 133, and look at the picture while counting to three. Then without looking back, quickly jot down answers to the following questions:

1. What was the picture about?
2. What did you see?
3. How many ducks were there?
4. How many white ducks?
5. What kinds of jackets were the people wearing?
6. Which person wore dark trousers?

Reflect for a moment on your answers. Chances are questions one and two presented no problems. But what about questions three and four, five and six? Most people can get a general impression of the photograph in a short time and clearly describe both the subject and action. Here is how one student answered.

1. The picture is about two people feeding ducks.
2. I saw people, ducks, water, trees, buildings.
3. Don't know.
4. Don't know.
5. Plaid?
6. Person on left?

Were your answers similar? Did you know *in general* what the picture was about, but were you unable to recall *specific* details? A quick glance revealed much information and you knew what the picture was about. By skimming the photograph, you *read* the large and central images, and the picture had meaning. To answer questions three and four, you would have to *reread* the picture. The choice of action would depend upon purposes: those of you who are curious may go back to count the ducks; others may not. However, if this were a test, everyone would count carefully for the correct answer. The same principle holds true in reading: the decision to skim or to read for detail depends on the purpose for reading. Nevertheless, skimming is not a substitute for closer or detailed reading. Each reading technique has a specific purpose and, as you will soon see, both are essential to academic work.

In academic work it is important to skim everything you read, then at a second reading, to scrutinize the material more closely. By following this approach, you separate and clearly differentiate among levels and gradations of ideas. As a result, the organization of a text stands out "in relief" as on a map that shows high and low altitudes of an area. In addition, the increased understanding of levels of ideas gives increased dimension and clarity to your own writing. The first application of skimming and free writing is for analysis and understanding of another writer's work. It is called "How to Assay an Essay."

HOW TO ASSAY AN ESSAY

An *assay* is a test made on a metal to analyze its composition and measure or extract its valuable metallic content. As readers, we examine a piece of writing in much the same manner as a metallurgist assays a metal. We analyze an essay for its thesis, concluding statement, and related ideas. We weigh and measure its content and form until we can extract the precious portion—its meaning. Until we analyze to understand its meaning, we cannot write critically or clearly about an author's work. The assaying of an essay is one way of extracting meaning for the purposes of clear understanding and critical writing. Read through the assay procedure which follows, and visualize yourself completing each step.

Preparation

Read the title and author's name.
Reflect briefly on both title and author.
Write freely, describing your expectations of the essay.
  1.   What does the title reveal?
  2.   Try to predict or anticipate some of the information that might be included in the essay.
  3.   What does the author's name or background (if known) suggest?
  4.   Try to predict the author's point of view or "slant" on the subject.

Step One: Recognizing
the Thesis

Read the essay until you come to the author's thesis: the *this is what I am going to say* statement.

Reflect: A thesis tells what the essay will be about. You may have to read one or more paragraphs to find it, but often it follows the introduction. Sometimes it is implied rather than stated. In that case, you may have to infer, or state the thesis in your own words, based on the author's statements.

1. Does the thesis you found tell what the essay will be about?
2. Does the thesis reveal something of the author's viewpoint, feeling, or attitude toward the subject?

Write down the thesis statement. Use the author's words if the thesis is stated; use your own words if it is implied.

If, in the first two paragraphs, there are no clues to the author's thesis, continue with the *assay* then, when you have completed step three, reread and complete step one.

Step Two: Recognizing
the Conclusion

Read the last paragraph of the essay for the author's concluding statement: *this is what I have said.*

Reflect: If the last paragraph does not reveal the summary or conclusion, read a paragraph or two before it until you find the concluding statement.

1. Does the statement summarize, conclude, or tell something about what was said?
2. Does the statement include the author's viewpoint or attitude toward the subject?

Write down the concluding statement. Use the author's words if the conclusion is explicit; use your own words if it is implied or suggested.

If, in the last two paragraphs, there are no clues to the author's conclusion, continue with the *assay* then, when you have completed step three, reread and complete this section.

Reread the thesis and the concluding statement.

Reflect: Is there a relationship between the two statements? Are they compatible or in agreement? Or, do they seem unrelated? Do they contain opposing or incompatible ideas?

If the statements seem to be unrelated or not complementary, reread the opening and closing paragraphs to reconsider your choices of thesis and conclusion. At this point, you may wish to choose another sentence for either the thesis or the conclusion. You may decide to change one or the other, or you may conclude that your original choices were best.

Write: If you have chosen or inferred another statement for the thesis or conclusion, write down your final choices.

Step Three: Recognizing Smaller, Related Ideas

Read the first sentence of each paragraph.

Reflect briefly on the sentence and its relationship to the thesis.

Write each of the sentences in the order of appearance, leaving four or five spaces on your paper between each sentence.

If you have not already done so, look up all words you do not understand or for which you cannot get meaning from the context of the sentences in which they appear.

Write one sentence in your own words to summarize or tell what the essay is about. *Remember, the summary will be written from the information included in the thesis, conclusion, and first sentences of each paragraph.*

If you have not, as yet, determined the author's thesis and/or conclusion, study the extracted sentences then reread and complete steps one and two.

Steps one through three of "How to Assay an Essay" provide an overview of an essay. Skimming the surface or reading only key portions gives a firm sense of an essay's thesis and related ideas. By reflecting, writing, and predicting, you add an even deeper dimension to the analysis of an author's work. As a reader, after completing an *assay*, you know what the piece is about, where the author begins, how far he or she develops the topic, and what he or she concludes. In fact, you will know enough about the essay to assure that later, at closer inspection, your familiarity with theme and central thoughts will increase immeasurably your overall understanding of the material. As a writer, your experience of the assay approach leads directly to an effective and proven strategy for developing an original topic, but before thinking about an original topic, apply the *assay* to another author's work.

INDEPENDENT ACTIVITY

Turn to page 132 and read "The Rhythms and Levels of Sleep" by Peter Farb using the step-by-step assay approach. Read only portions of the essay as directed. For example, do not be tempted to read beyond the first sentence of each paragraph. If you have never practiced skimming, you may find the discipline of limiting your reading to one sentence somewhat unnatural. Do not be concerned, simply remind yourself at each new paragraph to stop, write the sentence, and move on.

GROUP ACTIVITIES

Share the results of the *assay* of the Farb essay with the class or a small group.

Discuss choices of thesis and concluding statements.

Listen to others' choices and prepare to defend or argue against a choice of thesis or conclusion by referring to the essay itself for evidence.

Share and compare one-sentence summary statements.

How do summaries relate to thesis, conclusion, and the leading sentences of the essay's paragraphs?

What conclusions or generalizations can you draw from the group's discussion of the author's thesis, conclusion, and leading sentences?

HOW TO DEVELOP AN ESSAY

Now that you have gotten a firm grasp of an essay's thesis and related ideas, *without having read the whole essay*, you can get a firm grasp of central ideas for an original essay *before* completing the first draft. When you followed the *assay* steps, you analyzed "The Rhythms and Levels of Sleep" for both content (meaning) and form (structure). You searched first for the premise or basic idea of the essay, and you found at the start, the author's conclusion. In other words, you immediately got the whole picture, or *gestalt*. You watched the essay move from *A* to *Z*; then, by skimming first sentences of paragraphs, you saw *how* the author got from *A* to *Z*. You will develop your own essay in the same analytical way.

Because reading and writing are complementary processes, assaying and developing an essay are flip sides of the same coin. That is why the development of an original essay follows the same progression of steps as the *assay*. To put it simply, after deciding on a topic to write about, you will

1. formulate a thesis statement,
2. write a tentative conclusion,

3. subdivide the thesis into smaller, related ideas,

4. develop a paragraph for each of the related ideas.

To demonstrate with a familiar idea, turn to the chart in Chapter One where you were asked to think about beginnings, middles, and endings. Consider as your topic "A Meaningful Period." You are ahead of the game because you know how the period began and ended. Does that mean you have a thesis? No, not quite.

A thesis is a unique idea; it is not as broad a subject as "College," "Life," or "Working." Yet it is broader or larger than specific statements such as "College closed today because of snow," "He lives on Elm Street," "I want to work as a computer programmer." Somewhere between a broad, general topic and a narrow, specific statement lies the thesis. Moreover, a thesis is unique because it carries within it something of you, the writer. While the thesis is focusing on a smaller portion of a large topic, it is at the same time revealing *something* about the way the writer will deal with his or her portion of the topic.

Formulating a Thesis Statement

Reread what you wrote for "A Meaningful Period." You were asked to think of an event in your life that continued over an extended period of time. Your example may be similar to or quite different from one of these events:

1. My first month in college
2. The summer I worked at the supermarket
3. The first time I taught freshman English

Although the three events listed above narrow the topic "A Meaningful Period," and reveal something of *who* the writer is, they are not thesis statements. They are not thesis statements because they do not reveal *how* each writer perceived the event. Individuals' perceptions of events are so varied that a dozen people writing about each of the events would produce a dozen different thesis statements. Each writer, each person, comes from a different area or background and brings to an event his or her unique experiences and perceptions about life. A perfect example is the variety of answers a police officer may get from witnesses to an accident. Each witness views the incident from *a different angle of vision*. A thesis statement reveals an author's angle of vision or slant on the subject. It is, in essence, the author's stand *in favor of* or *against* an issue, or an author's personal and unique feelings and impressions *about* a subject. As readers, we are free to agree or disagree with a writer's thesis. As writers, we must give our reader something to agree or disagree with.

INDEPENDENT ACTIVITIES

A THESIS WORKSHEET

Read the beginning, middle, and ending of your chart for "A Meaningful Period."

Reflect on the extended period by answering the following questions:
1. *What* happened? *Who* was present?
2. *Where* and *When* did the event or period take place?
3. *Why* did it happen?
4. *How* do I feel about the experience?

Write freely in answer to each question. Jot down thoughts randomly and quickly, as they occur.

Here are examples of thesis worksheets for the three events mentioned earlier.

MY FIRST MONTH IN COLLEGE

1. was homesick
   had a roommate who smoked
   learned to like institutional food
   had trouble with math, liked psychology
   made many friends
   began to *think* more
   realized I have come a long way—also, I have a long way to go.
2. on campus
   September-October
3. I chose it—was ready for it—independence
4. I recommend it even for the timid and shy.

THE SUMMER I WORKED AT THE SUPERMARKET

1. It was hot—a mixture of smells
   saw so many different kinds of people coming through the checkout
   got tired a lot—feet hurt
   learned to save *some* money
   met *someone*
2. at the supermarket
   July-August
3. I needed the money for college—spending money
   needed someone to talk to, to care about, to write home to—from college
4. doesn't matter where you work when you meet someone you like a lot

THE FIRST TIME I TAUGHT FRESHMAN ENGLISH

1. wasn't sure how to approach the subject—until I met the students; each one was so different
   I took an entirely new approach to teaching—free writing to which I responded each day; students liked it; they talked about many things; we all felt good about it;
   students' reading and writing improved
2. on campus, September
3. I wanted to teach writing; loved writing as well as reading, although I frequently looked for excuses to avoid the hard work involved in writing
4. It was my most satisfying teaching experience.
   I discovered that *every* student is capable of improving reading and writing skills—even those whose native language is not English—and particularly those who come to college with little experience in extended writing and reading.

Read the following thesis statements which writers of the three thesis worksheets might have composed. Rate each thesis statement on a scale of one to three: Give a score of *one* to the statement that contains all or most of the necessary elements of a thesis; give a score of *three* to the statement that contains the lowest number of elements; give a score of *two* to the statement that falls somewhere between the best thesis statement (1) and the least effective (3).

Reflect on the criteria (below) for judging the effectiveness of each thesis statement.

Thesis statement is not too general, not too specific.

Thesis statement focuses on a smaller portion of a large topic.

Thesis statement reveals something of the author's view on the subject.

Thesis statement can be subdivided into smaller, related ideas.

Rate each thesis statement: 1 = most effective; 3 = least effective; 2 = moderately effective.

MY FIRST MONTH IN COLLEGE

a. College made me homesick and hateful of smokers._____
b. College offers a variety of new experiences for those who are ready to learn, grow, and bend._____
c. My first month in college taught me to avoid math courses, to like institutional food, and to make friends._____

THE SUMMER I WORKED AT THE SUPERMARKET

a. It doesn't matter where you work in the summer if you have a good reason for working._____

b. The supermarket attracts all kinds of people._____

c. Meeting someone you really like can change the way you look at a difficult job, sore feet, and a changing future._____

THE FIRST TIME I TAUGHT FRESHMAN ENGLISH

a. Each semester of teaching is a new and different experience._____

b. Teaching freshman composition taught *me* much about writing._____

c. Responding to my students' writing each day helped to improve my own writing skills, increased my reading rate, and made me a better teacher._____

Reread your thesis worksheet for "A Meaningful Period."

Reflect on a possible thesis statement; use the same criteria on your own thesis as you used to rate the three thesis statements in the preceding activity.

Write a thesis statement that would get a *one* rating.

GROUP ACTIVITIES

Share with the class or a small group your ratings of the statements in the preceding activity.

Discuss reasons for your choices of ratings.

Listen to others' reasons for choices of ratings.

Argue, if you feel strongly, for or against a number *one* rating until the group reaches a consensus. The majority should agree, at least on the top-rated thesis in each of the three categories.

Read your original thesis statement aloud for group discussion. Refer to criteria for thesis statements during the discussion.

Reflect on the group's discussion of your thesis.

Write a revised thesis statement in light of the group discussion.

Writing A Tentative Conclusion

Student writers frequently complain of not being able to stick to a subject or of going off in different directions. Their papers often are marked *rambling, strays from topic,* or *not related to thesis.* As readers, these same students may have the parallel problem of losing track of a topic as they read. Their minds tend to wander from the text, and after reading, they cannot recall what a chapter was about. Without a specific technique to tackle the problem, wandering worsens as reading and writing assignments get heavier. The solutions to the wandering problems of both reader and writer are contained in this section. Wandering is solved by the careful *assay* of an author's essay and the parallel development of an original essay.

The direct progression from thesis to conclusion in the *assay* of "The Rhythms and Levels of Sleep" gave you, the reader, an immediate sense of the *limits* set by the author on the essay. As a writer, when you compose a tentative conclusion immediately after writing a thesis statement, you too set limits on the direction of your writing.

The method is similar to putting your car in cruise mode set at fifty-five miles an hour and taking your foot off the gas pedal. You continue to direct, steer, and control the automobile, but you are confident that the limit will be maintained. As a result, the *limitation* on your car's speed *frees* you from watching the speedometer, worrying about getting a speeding ticket, and developing a cramp in your right leg. Furthermore, you know you can step on the gas or brake pedal if you choose to change speed or to lift the limit entirely. Similarly, when you write an essay, setting limits on your topic allows you the freedom of writing quickly, thinking sharply, and sticking to your subject.

INDEPENDENT ACTIVITIES

Read once more your thesis statement for "A Meaningful Period." *Reflect* on the ideas contained in the statement.

Write a tentative concluding statement for your proposed essay. In other words, *predict* from your thesis how you might conclude your essay.

While you are working with the beginning and ending of your proposed essay, write a tentative title as well. A title should be short and eye-catching and should clearly reflect the content of your thesis.

When you are satisfied with your thesis and conclusion, you are ready to subdivide the thesis into smaller, related ideas.

Subdividing A Thesis into Smaller, Related Ideas

If a diagram were drawn describing what you have done thus far in developing your essay, it would shape up like the diagram presented in Figure 4-1.

```
┌──────────────────────────────────────────────────────┐
│   TITLE                                                │
│                               Title written            │
└──────────────────────────────────────────────────────┘

┌──────────────────────────────────────────────────────┐
│   FIRST PARAGRAPH (s)                                  │
│                               Thesis statement written │
└──────────────────────────────────────────────────────┘

┌──────────────────────────────────────────────────────┐
│   MIDDLE PARAGRAPHS                                    │
│                                                        │
│                                                        │
│                                                        │
│                                                        │
│                                                        │
│                                                        │
│                                                        │
│                                                        │
└──────────────────────────────────────────────────────┘

┌──────────────────────────────────────────────────────┐
│   LAST PARAGRAPH (s)                                   │
│                               Conclusion written       │
└──────────────────────────────────────────────────────┘
```

FIGURE 4-1

If a diagram were drawn to describe "The Rhythms and Levels of Sleep" by Peter Farb, it would look like the diagram shown in Figure 4-2.

The obvious difference between Farb's and your diagram is in the middle paragraphs' portion. Farb's thesis has been subdivided into smaller, related ideas which have become first sentences of paragraphs in the middle portion of the essay.

One way of subdividing a statement into separate, meaningful segments is by asking direct questions, such as

Who or *What* is (are) the subject(s)?
[Subjects are the persons, places, things, or ideas an author mentions.]

What is (are) the subject(s) doing?
When or *Where* does the action take place?
Why or *How* does the action occur?

TITLE: The Rhythms and Levels of Sleep

FIRST PARAGRAPH (s)

   Thesis: Scientists now know that the sleeping brain is as active as the waking one, and that at certain times during the sleep period it is furiously at work in the processing of information.

MIDDLE PARAGRAPHS

1. Scientists do not even know how much sleep people need.

2. Sleep researchers have so far failed to answer fully . . .

3. If sleep does not serve an absolutely vital function . . .

4. The modern understanding of sleep began quite by . . .

5. A number of curious experiences occur at the onset of sleep.

6. The first period of sleep is always NREM.

7. The new view of sleep that has emerged in the past . . .

8. REM sleep, in contrast, apparently restores the neural processes underlying consciousness; it is mental rather than . . .

LAST PARAGRAPH(s)

   Conclusion: Such experiments offer fresh evidence that sleep is one of the most active parts of a person's day.

FIGURE 4-2

Farb's thesis, subdivided into segments, may look like any one of the following diagrams:

Scientists		know
Sleeping brain		is as active
		as waking one
	and at certain times during sleep period	
		is furiously at work in the processing of information.

Scientists		sleeping brain
know		is active as waking one
	[and at certain times during sleep period]	
		is furiously at work in the processing of information.

Scientists	sleeping brain	sleep period
know	is active as waking one	at certain times during. . .
	is furiously at work in the processing of information	

The point of showing three different, yet not so different, ways of breaking down a statement into its meaningful segments is this: As long as the subdivisions make sense to you, it doesn't matter how you divide the statement. The important thing is to see clearly the elements of a particular thesis and to know that each element *must* be considered and expanded in the essay. If a subject included in a thesis is *never* mentioned in the essay, the writer betrays his or her commitment to the reader.

A thesis is a commitment.

Read the following three thesis statements and subdivide each into its meaningful segments. Diagram the divisions. Write a concluding statement and a title for each one.

1. College offers a variety of new experiences for those who are ready to learn, grow, and bend.
2. Meeting someone you really like can change the way you look at a difficult job, sore feet, and a changing future.
3. Responding to my students' writing each day helped me to improve my own writing skills, increased my reading rate, and made me a better teacher.

Reflect on your thesis for "A Meaningful Period."

Write your thesis statement in *chart* form, as you did in the preceding exercise, by dividing your thesis into segments or smaller, related ideas, which you will expand into paragraphs later on when writing the first draft of your essay.

SUMMARY

Pre-reading/writing, through the use of skimming and free writing, isolates key portions of a text and generates key ideas for an original essay. By providing the reader/writer with a sense of wholeness or *gestalt*, this stage is preparation for a closer inspection of a text and for the writing of a first draft of an original essay.

INDEPENDENT ACTIVITIES

Read your chart which subdivides the elements of your thesis for "A Meaningful Period."

Reflect on all of the elements.

Write freely and separately about each meaningful segment, adding facts, memories, people, places, and ideas that relate specifically to the segment. The material generated by this exercise will grow into the sentences and paragraphs of your essay.

Assay "Reading Passage Number One" on page 126.

Diagram the passage as the Farb piece is diagrammed on page 57.

Review your Reading Log. How is it coming along? What is happening to your reading habits? Write a short summary of what has happened thus far. Think about the next book you will choose to read.

Review your Daily Journal. Write a short summary to describe what has happened to your writing or feelings about writing since you began the journal.

GROUP ACTIVITIES

Share with the class or small group your charts and diagrams depicting subdivisions of the three thesis statements on page 59. In addition, share your personal thesis statement and chart.

Discuss personal thesis statement diagrams at length to verify, through feedback from an audience, the relationship among subdivisions and thesis.

Listen to others' thesis statements and charts to spark ideas and approaches which you may wish to experiment with.

HOW TO USE THE ASSAY METHOD TO CAPTURE THE MEANING OF A TEXTBOOK CHAPTER

Textbook chapters make up the bulk of academic reading; therefore, you need a proven method for getting key ideas quickly before taking a closer look at details. Studies have shown that prereading for central concepts increases overall comprehension of a text. Furthermore, the combination of skimming and free writing can have an even more powerful effect on your understanding of a chapter. With minor modifications, the *assay* is readily adapted to chapter reading.

Chapters differ from essays in length, degrees of technicality, and form. Generally, a chapter is longer and contains more technical material than an essay. The form or structure of a chapter, however, varies. At first glance certain chapters in the social sciences might be indistinguishable from essays. But on closer inspection, the large amount of factual material, the lack of opinion, and the impersonal style clearly identify the chapter.

Other differences include purpose, audience, and tone. The purpose of a chapter is to instruct, and it is written for a specific audience—students. Although they may also instruct, essays more often inform or entertain and can be written either for particular audiences or the general reader. An essay's tone may vary from high humor to dead seriousness, while a chapter's tone tends to be more formal and objective. Yet it too may vary in its degree of formality. These differences, while not startling, demand a slightly different prereading approach.

Preparation

Read the chapter's title, subtitles, and headings. Glance at charts and diagrams; read their titles or headings.

Reflect on what you have read.

Write one sentence in which you anticipate or *predict* what the chapter will be about.

Step One: Recognizing the Chapter's Purpose

Read the beginning paragraph(s) for a statement of purpose or thesis (this is what the chapter will be about).

Reflect: Is there a statement that tells what the chapter is about?

Write down the statement, or use your own words.

If a statement of purpose is not evident, go to step two.

Step Two: Recognizing the Conclusion

Read the last paragraph or two for a concluding statement; read the end-of-chapter questions or exercises.

Reflect on the questions; this is the information you are to recall.

Write the conclusion or summary statement as written, or in your own words.

If a conclusion is not evident, go to step three.

Step Three: Recognizing Smaller, Related Ideas

Read headings and first sentences of each paragraph.

Reflect briefly on the relationship of heading to first sentences.

Write headings and first sentences in order of appearance. Indent first sentences and leave four or five spaces between each.

If you have not done so, look up all words you do not understand or for which you cannot get meaning from the context. Check the textbook glossary before looking in the dictionary.

Write two or three sentences to summarize or tell what the chapter is about.

If purpose statement and/or conclusion have not been determined, study the extracted sentences. Then reread and complete steps one and two.

INDEPENDENT ACTIVITIES

Use the *Assay* method to capture the meaning of the chapter excerpt entitled "States of Awareness" page 136.

Complete all chapter assignments in other subjects the same way.

Jot down specific successes, problems, or differences you encounter (when reading textbook chapters) in the sciences, social sciences, and other subjects.

Prepare to discuss your findings with the class or a small group.

five

Reading/Writing:
Inferential Reasoning

Now that you have your thesis, conclusion, and related ideas for "A Meaningful Period," you have the bare bones, or *skeleton*, of an outline for an original essay. You are to be congratulated. Writers often feel "blocked," or unable to write, until they achieve this. You, however, have succeeded in organizing thoughts and ideas clearly and logically into a blueprint for an essay.

It is most important to remember that the blueprint is yours: your ideas, your thoughts, your labor. As you work to refine your essay, you can change anything and everything. As you gather new information, as you write, think, and read, you can alter, delete, or add to the original plan. You may totally revise or reverse your thesis and conclusion. In other words, do not expect the final draft to resemble the first. And when you write your first draft, it may very well look something like the manuscript shown in Figure 5-1.

Writing is a process, not a formula, and although techniques presented here are structured and may appear formulated, they are not. Each method is geared to release your writing abilities and reading

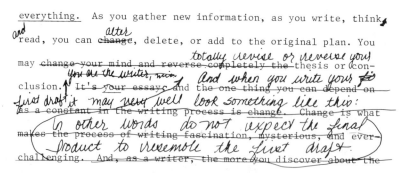

FIGURE 5-1

strengths and, while you are learning new strategies, to free you from the constraints of having to deal with organization, process, and comprehension simultaneously. You will find that each writing/reading task demands a slightly different approach. Those taught here work best in situations where you are under the pressures of time constraints and work deadlines—which may be forever.

WHAT CAN YOU EXPECT
FROM THIS CHAPTER

The second phase of the reading/writing process is a practicing stage. During this phase you, as reader/writer, will apply the basic principles of paragraph development to "fill in" those spaces between central ideas in your essay, and to recognize practices used by experienced writers to "fill out" their skeletal writing plans. You will practice *inferential reasoning.* You will see relationships among ideas, make comparisons, draw conclusions, infer, and generalize. You will learn to recognize and write paragraphs using these reasoning skills. You will learn to build up to a thesis statement and to work down to a conclusion. You will understand why you wrote the thesis and conclusion first, why you subdivided your thesis into smaller, related ideas, and why you will read an essay or chapter in a similar way.

Chapter Five introduces *moderate reading speed* and *focused writing* as ways of taking a closer look at a text or an original essay in progress. The chapter takes you step by step through procedures that lead to increased comprehension of reading material and clearer understanding of writing techniques. This chapter comes into focus best when you use moderate reading speed and focused writing for completing assignments in other subjects, for listening more effectively in class, and for studying more efficiently at home.

MODERATE READING SPEED
AND FOCUSED WRITING

Moderate reading speed is used for examining the details of a chapter or essay by paying close attention to the author's use of subdivisions or paragraphs. It is slower than the general reading rate you calculated earlier (Chapter Two). Moderate reading conditions include the times you are neither skimming at a fast clip for central ideas, nor studying at a deliberate pace for an examination, yet want to read in a focused way for a close look at details.

Focused writing is a way of developing a first draft of an original piece of writing, paragraph by paragraph, without losing the spontaneity of free writing and discovery. It is a way of planning for details without the rigid structure of a formal outline. Because first drafts entail thinking through ideas, focused writing is accomplished at a slower pace than free writing, yet at a faster rate than rewriting (Chapter Six).

Focused writing and moderate reading speed are complementary processes: focused writing enables you to expand upon your original thesis statement and smaller, related ideas; moderate reading speed helps you to see how an author expands and develops a thesis and smaller, related ideas.

THE POWER OF FOCUSING

The power of focusing can be demonstrated by taking a closer look at the photograph in the appendix (page 126). When you glanced at it the first time (Chapter Four), you got a *general* idea of what the picture was about but did not have enough time to study or to focus on *specific* details. Look at the picture again, thinking about the answers to those questions you were not able to answer at first glance: *What was the picture about? What did you see? How many ducks were there? How many white ducks? What kinds of jackets were the people wearing? Which person wore dark trousers?*

With enough time for a second look, you can answer all the questions. The same principle holds true in reading and writing. Skimming and free writing are accomplished quickly to reveal or to develop *general* or global ideas. On the other hand, reading for details and writing a first draft are accomplished at a moderate pace to reveal or develop *specific* supporting details.

FOCUSING ON DETAILS:
THE PARAGRAPH

Reading for details requires knowledge of paragraph construction. In order to focus on the paragraph, you, as reader, must keep in mind that a paragraph is a group of sentences developing a single or *guiding idea*.

The guiding idea often is expressed in one of the paragraph's sentences; it is the topic of that sentence. In this text, the sentence containing the guiding idea will be called the *guiding sentence*. The term *guiding* is used because, in addition to revealing the idea, subject, or topic of the paragraph, the guiding sentence literally guides (and limits) the subject matter of all the other sentences in the paragraph. In effect, all other sentences in the paragraph must make statements about the idea in the guiding sentence. Put another way, all other sentences in a paragraph *expand* upon the guiding idea.

Authors expand upon guiding ideas in a number of ways. For academic purposes and analytical writing, ways of expanding ideas can be divided into three broad classifications: *Addition, Analysis,* and *Argument.* With few exceptions, most of what a writer does with supporting sentences in informative paragraphs can be classified as *Adding* information, *Analyzing* information, or *Arguing* for or against a point of information. *Sentences that add* supply more information about the guiding idea through example, illustration, description, or definition. One way to compose sentences that add information is to ask yourself *Who? What? When?* and *Where?* questions. The answers to the questions become statements that support the guiding idea.

Sentences that analyze expand a guiding idea by showing relationships between or among ideas, events, or people. One way to show relationships is to ask yourself *how* or *why* questions: How are things similar or different? How did an incident or act cause something else to happen? How or why were others affected by the incident or act? In what ways were the effects felt? How significant were the effects?

Sentences that argue may support or deny a guiding idea through a particular point of view, judgment, or criticism. The writer, depending upon the subject and nature of the work, defends or judges events, acts, or ideas from a personal point of view, or from another viewpoint. A book reviewer, for example, will use both a personal viewpoint and literary criteria to judge a book. A term paper writer will quote from researched sources, experts in the field, or news reports to support statements, a thesis, or a point of view. Essays express personal viewpoints, while textbooks present factual material. Books containing political or controversial subjects may explore one side of an issue or, on the other hand, may present a complete picture of an argument.

As you examine paragraphs from the perspective of a reader/writer, you will find few *pure* paragraphs. *Pure* means paragraphs in which all sentences either add information, analyze, or argue. Most paragraphs contain a mixture or blend of idea-expanding sentences. Indeed, some sentences themselves, may analyze, add information, and argue at the same time. The multiplicity of idea expanders makes for more interesting paragraphs; however, there are exceptions. In the social sciences, for instance, an entire chapter may be devoted to defining a complex concept or to arguing for or against a case. In the technical sciences, a description of a process or procedure may run for many pages. In political writing, argument as an idea expander may predominate.

All paragraphs, pure or mixed, answer questions for the reader. As the writer, you must predict what the reader might ask and when the reader might ask it. Predicting questions a reader might ask is easier to understand if you think of each paragraph as a short conversation between two people who meet on a street. Imagine meeting an acquaintance who greets you unemotionally with, "Jeremiah is dead," and walks on. Now that is a guiding idea if you've ever heard one. You are left with many questions: *What? What was that? Will you repeat that, please? When did he die? How? Where? Who's Jeremiah?* Although conversation and writing are different, both in tone and form, a poor or underdeveloped paragraph is as frustrating for the reader as an incomplete conversation is for the listener.

An underdeveloped, partial, or incomplete paragraph contains unfinished thoughts, illogical sequences of ideas, and leaves the reader dissatisfied. A dissatisfied reader either stops reading, or demands answers to questions such as *Where's the proof? When are you going to get to the point? Why should I accept that statement when you offer nothing to support it? So what? Who cares?*

A developed, whole, or complete paragraph contains finished thoughts, logical sequences of ideas, and leaves the reader satisfied. A satisfied reader gets answers to questions he or she did not know enough to ask until the writer brought up the subject. Effective writers offer answers to questions they themselves might ask as readers. Effective readers become effective writers when they recognize and understand the use of guiding ideas in paragraph development.

Recognizing:

Guiding Ideas
Guiding Sentences
Idea-Expanding Sentences

You can immediately see how an author expands a guiding idea into a sentence, then into a paragraph, by answering the following questions:

1. What is the paragraph's guiding idea?
2. What statement does the author make about the guiding idea (in the guiding sentence)?
3. How does the author expand upon the guiding idea in each of the other sentences in the paragraph?
   a. Do the sentences add, analyze, or argue?
   b. What does the author say about the guiding idea in the sentence?

Look at the second paragraph from Peter Farb's essay, "The Rhythms and Levels of Sleep." Assume, as you did when *skimming*, that the first sentence is the guiding sentence, then ask the questions.

> Scientists do not even know how much sleep people need. A generation ago, most hygiene books stated that adults require eight hours of sleep each night. Sleep researchers are now discovering, though, that the amount of sleep needed is very much an individual matter. Cases are known of extremely active people who for half a century never slept more than four hours a night. On the other hand, even a healthy person may need as much as seventeen hours on occasion. Claims have been made from time to time concerning people who supposedly went for extremely long periods with no sleep at all, but most such cases never survived scientific scrutiny. The longest verified case on record is that of a high-school youth who was kept under constant observation by researchers from the Stanford University Sleep Laboratory, and who stayed awake for 264 consecutive hours—exactly eleven days—without exhibiting any serious emotional changes. In fact, he remained so alert that on the last night of his vigil he beat one of the researchers in every game they played in a penny arcade. Nor did he exhibit any exceptional need to make up sleep afterward. Following the first sleep lasting only about fourteen hours, he stayed up for 24 hours before going to sleep again, this time for a mere eight hours.[1]

If the first sentence is the guiding sentence of the paragraph, the three questions could be answered in the following way:

1. What is the paragraph's guiding idea?
    Answer: the amount of sleep people need
2. What statement does the author make about the guiding idea (in the guiding sentence)?
    Answer: scientists do not even know how much sleep people need
3. How does the author expand upon the guiding idea in each of the other sentences in the paragraph?
    a. Does the sentence add, analyze, or argue?
    b. What does the author say about the guiding idea in the sentence?

ANSWERS

Second sentence	a. adds information
	b. we used to think people needed eight hours
Third sentence	a. adds information
	b. amount needed is an individual matter
Fourth sentence	a. adds information
	b. some people need only four hours
Fifth sentence	a. adds information, analyzes (comparison)
	b. some may need seventeen hours

[1]From *Humankind* by Peter Farb. Copyright © 1978 by Peter Farb. Reprinted by permission of Houghton Mifflin Company and Jonathan Cape Limited.

Sixth sentence	a. adds information, analyzes (comparison) b. some went long periods with no sleep
Seventh sentence	a. adds information, analyzes (contrast, cause) b. one student stayed awake eleven days
Eighth sentence	a. adds information, analyzes (effect) b. remained alert despite lack of sleep
Ninth sentence	a. analyzes (effect) b. had no need to make up sleep missed
Tenth sentence	a. analyzes (results) b. quickly returned to normal sleep pattern

It is clear that each sentence in Farb's second paragraph contains a reference to the guiding idea, thus confirming the original assumption that the first sentence is the guiding sentence.

A safe rule to follow is: test the first sentence of the paragraph for the guiding idea. Then, if the majority of the sentences do *not* refer to your chosen guiding sentence, you will have to look elsewhere in the paragraph for the guiding idea. The guiding sentence will become evident as you test the other sentences.

Examine the following paragraphs, assuming again that the first sentence contains the guiding idea, and answer the questions.

Farb: Paragraph Five

A number of curious experiences occur at the onset of sleep. A person just about to go to sleep may experience an electric shock, a flash of light, or a crash of thunder—but the most common sensation is that of floating or falling, which is why "falling asleep" is a scientifically valid description. A nearly universal occurrence at the beginning of sleep (although not everyone recalls it) is a sudden, uncoordinated jerk of the head, the limbs, or even the entire body. Most people tend to think of going to sleep as a slow slippage into oblivion, but the onset of sleep is not gradual at all. It happens in an instant. One moment the individual is awake, the next moment not.[2]

1. What is the paragraph's guiding idea? _____

_____

2. What statement does the author make about the guiding idea (in the guiding sentence)? _____

_____

3. How does the author expand upon the guiding idea in each of the other sentences in the paragraph?
   a. Does the sentence add, analyze, or argue?
   b. What does the author say about the guiding idea in the sentence?

[2]From *Humankind* by Peter Farb. Copyright © 1978 by Peter Farb. Reprinted by permission of Houghton Mifflin Company and Jonathan Cape Limited.

ANSWERS

Second sentence   a. _____

                      b. _____

Third sentence   a. _____

                      b. _____

Fourth sentence   a. _____

                      b. _____

Fifth sentence   a. _____

                      b. _____

Conclusion: First sentence is _____ , is not _____ the guid-
                      ing sentence.

Farb: Paragraph Seven

The new view of sleep that has emerged in the past few decades from numerous laboratories is not one of sleep as "death's counterfeit," as Shakespeare put it. Sleep is not passive in the sense that it is the absence of something characteristic of wakefulness. Rather, it is an active state in which the brain is never at rest. One theory about human sleep assigns different functions to the two kinds of sleep. NREM sleep apparently does the things that have traditionally been assigned by common sense to all sleep: growth, repair to the body's tissues, and the synthesis of proteins. NREM sleep is a biological necessity; without it, an individual eventually would collapse. When someone is deprived of sleep, NREM sleep is usually made up first. And until the deprivation is compensated for, that person feels lethargic and less able than usual to carry out physical tasks.[3]

1. What is the paragraph's guiding idea? _____

   _____

2. What statement does the author make about the guiding idea (in the guiding sentence)? _____

   _____

3. How does the author expand upon the guiding idea in each of the other sentences in the paragraph?
   a. Does the sentence add, analyze, or argue?
   b. What does the author say about the guiding idea in the sentence?

[3]From *Humankind* by Peter Farb. Copyright © 1978 by Peter Farb. Reprinted by permission of Houghton Mifflin Company and Jonathan Cape Limited.

ANSWERS

Second sentence   a. _____

                      b. _____

Third sentence   a. _____

                      b. _____

Fourth sentence   a. _____

                      b. _____

Fifth sentence   a. _____

                      b. _____

Sixth sentence   a. _____

                      b. _____

Seventh sentence   a. _____

                      b. _____

Eighth sentence   a. _____

                      b. _____

Conclusion: The first sentence is _____ , is not _____ the
                      guiding sentence.

FOCUSING ON DETAILS:
THE FIRST DRAFT

Recognizing guiding ideas, guiding sentences, and idea-expanding sentences is the key to writing a focused first draft of an original essay. Writing a first draft is hard work. Although it may get easier with daily writing practice, it nevertheless always requires time for the sustained act of putting words on paper, one following another. Each writer works differently. One may begin a task by writing a full first draft which, when completed, is cut, rearranged, and outlined; another may prepare meticulous, detailed outlines before putting the first word on paper. Many writers do not stick to any *one* way of working. Sometimes they outline carefully; other times they begin with a first draft. Often, writers work intensively on single segments of a longer piece of writing, reorganizing later, when all the segments are completed. Most writers agree that at some time during the writing of an essay or chapter, they have to deal individually with each and every paragraph. Paying close attention to guiding ideas, guiding sentences, and idea-expanding sentences is one way of dealing with paragraphs.

You have already generated smaller, related ideas for your essay, "A Meaningful Period." Each one of those smaller ideas can become the guiding idea for a paragraph. As the writer, you may build a paragraph from a guiding idea in any number of ways. With practice you will discover the approach that works best for you. The three approaches that are about to be described are by no means the only ways of developing paragraphs. They are, however, techniques that are known to work.

Writing:

Guiding Ideas
Guiding Sentences
Idea-Expanding Sentences

The *First Approach* is a structured one, and deals individually with each related idea. Take one of your smaller ideas and turn it into a guiding sentence. Then expand on the guiding sentence by writing three or four related sentences. *As the reader*, look at your completed paragraph objectively by asking, "What is the paragraph's guiding idea? What statement am I making about the guiding idea (in the guiding sentence)?" *As the writer*, expand further upon the ideas by asking, "How do I expand upon the guiding idea in each of the other sentences in the paragraph?" Repeat the process for each of the smaller, related ideas.

The *Second Approach* is somewhat less structured than the first. Take one of the smaller, related ideas from "A Meaningful Period," and free write about the idea until you can think of no more to say. Then, *as the reader*, look at your collection of sentences and ask, "What is the paragraph's guiding idea? What statement am I making about the guiding idea (in the guiding sentence)?" *As the writer*, ask yourself if you can further expand upon the idea through addition, analysis, or argument. Repeat the process for each smaller, related idea.

The *Third Approach* is less structured than either the first or second. In it, you simply reflect on your thesis, then write everything you can think of about the thesis. When you can write no more, go back, *as the reader*, and classify the material written under each of the smaller, related ideas. If your writing generated new ideas, use them as separate classifications. From each classification develop a paragraph. *As the writer*, ask the three questions about each completed paragraph.

As you have probably noticed, there are similarities as well as differences among the three approaches to paragraph development. One approach may seem more appealing than another. Try one, try them all, or take portions from each and put them together to develop your own approach. As you try your hand at different ways of expanding ideas into paragraphs, do not *rigidly* concern yourself with question three, *How* does the author expand upon the guiding idea? Experienced writers, while writing, are aware that they may be adding, analyzing, or arguing, yet are more likely to ask questions such as, "Does the paragraph stick to the point (my thesis)?" "Do the sentences stick to the point (my guiding idea)?" "Have I given the reader enough information to make my point clear?" "Will the reader have unanswered questions?" As you gain experience in expanding ideas into paragraphs, you will find that every approach works better when you ask questions from both the reader's and the writer's perspective.

OPENING AND CLOSING PARAGRAPHS

Opening and closing paragraphs are unique and have different purposes than middle paragraphs. This is why reader and writer must deal separately with introductory and concluding paragraphs. *As the reader*, when practicing skimming (Chapter Four), you read the opening paragraph(s) for the author's thesis, and you read the closing paragraph(s) for the author's summary. *As the writer*, you will build to your thesis statement in the opening paragraph(s), and you will work down to a conclusion in the closing paragraph(s). If you think of the thesis as the guiding idea of the introductory paragraph(s), and of the summary as the guiding idea for the closing paragraph(s), the connections between paragraphs and idea development will become clear. Just as each idea in a paragraph is related to the guiding idea, and each guiding idea is related to the thesis, all other ideas within an essay or chapter have connections as well. Good opening and closing paragraphs help the reader to see these connections among ideas.

Opening paragraphs introduce the reader to the subject. Reading an opening paragraph of text is similar to entering the front door of a house—the reader always has the option of turning around and leaving if there is nothing of interest. That is why the writer, to create a sense of expectation, uses ideas that build to the thesis.

Methods of building to a thesis are numerous. Writers build interest by asking or answering questions, making humorous or deadly serious observations, quoting a famous person, or defining a technical term.

Closing paragraphs gently move the reader out of the subject's frame of reference. Readers tend to favor endings in which all loose ends are tied up and all remaining questions are answered. That is why the writer carefully works down to the final statements.

Methods of working down to a conclusion include a restatement of the thesis (in different words), a summary of guiding ideas, an attempt to convince the reader of the importance of the thesis and supporting details, or a final thought-provoking question. Frequently a writer, to enhance an ending that may have grown dull from restatement, will add a new, but related, fact to the last paragraph.

Just as the entry and exit areas of a home differ from the interior rooms, so do the first and last paragraphs differ from the middle paragraphs of an essay or chapter. Begin now to look for and take note of effective introductions and conclusions in magazines, newspaper articles, and textbook chapters. An awareness of experienced writers' techniques will help you write more effective opening and closing paragraphs.

SUMMARY

Reading/writing, through moderate reading speed and focused writing, enables you to see how an author expands ideas into well-developed paragraphs and, at the same time, helps you to expand smaller, related ideas into effective paragraphs.

INDEPENDENT ACTIVITIES

I. Choose one or more of the following approaches (A, B, or C) to write your first draft for "A Meaningful Period."
    A. *Reread* your smaller, related ideas.
        Reflect on how each idea may become a guiding sentence.
        Write a guiding sentence for each idea.
        Reflect on each guiding sentence.
        Write three or four sentences expanding each of the guiding sentences into a paragraph.
        Reflect to choose a logical order for the sentences in each paragraph.
        Ask, for each paragraph, "What is my guiding idea? What am I saying about the guiding idea in the guiding sentence? Do each of the other sentences expand upon the guiding idea?"
    B. *Reflect* on one of the smaller, related ideas.
        Write about it until you cannot think of anything else to say.
        Read your draft.
        Reflect to choose a logical order for the sentences, and develop a paragraph for each related idea.
        Ask, for each paragraph, "What is the guiding idea? What do I say about the guiding idea? Does each of the other sentences expand upon the guiding idea?"
    C. *Read* your thesis, conclusion, and related ideas.
        Reflect on the thesis statement.

Write about the thesis until you can write no more.

Reread your material and classify the information under the appropriate smaller, related idea. If you find new ideas, group them into new classifications.

Reflect to choose a logical order for the sentences, and develop at least one paragraph for each idea.

Ask, for each paragraph, "What is my guiding idea? What do I say about the guiding idea in the guiding sentence? How does each of the other sentences expand upon the guiding idea?"

II. When you have completed one of the approaches (A, B, or C) for writing your first draft of "A Meaningful Period," it is time to think about your opening and closing paragraphs.

A. *Read* through your first draft of middle paragraphs.

Reflect on ways of introducing your subject to a reader.

Write an introductory paragraph in which you lead up or build to your thesis in a way that might hold a reader's interest.

Reread the introductory paragraph. Work on it until you are pleased with it.

B. *Read* your introduction and middle paragraphs.

Reflect on ways of bringing your essay to a conclusion.

Write a closing paragraph in which you restate the thesis, summarize the smaller ideas, or add a new thought-provoking question or statement.

Reread the concluding paragraph. Work on it until you are pleased with it.

III. Now that you have a completed first draft for "A Meaningful Period," it is time to look at it from a different perspective.

Read the draft from beginning to end.

Reflect on the following questions.

Write a few words in answer to the questions.

1. What are the strengths of this first draft? Place a check mark next to the portion you think is well done.
2. What are the weaknesses of this draft? Place an *X* next to the portion you think needs improvement.
3. How much revision or rewriting is needed?
4. How would I go about revising or improving this draft? Make a list of the strategies you might use to revise the essay.

Collect all your notes for "A Meaningful Period." Clip them together with the first draft and your answers to these questions. Put them in a folder or envelope, and put it aside. Get into the habit of keeping jottings, drafts, and source materials for a project in one folder or envelope that is clearly labelled. While you are performing other tasks and duties, ideas about the subject will occur to you. When this happens, write the new information on a piece of paper and slip the paper into the appropriate folder. This is a method used by professional writers, one which ensures that good ideas will not get away.

IV. Skim through some of your favorite magazines and collect at least three different kinds of openings or leads for articles. Do the same for conclusions. Plan to talk about them in your class or small group.

V. Highlight or underline the guiding sentences of each paragraph in the selections, "Without My Eights Hours I'm Type A" (page 144) and "RX for Depression: A Wake-up Call" (page 145).

GROUP ACTIVITIES

Share one or more of your paragraphs from "A Meaningful Period" with the class or a small group.

Listen to others' paragraphs.

Discuss one another's paragraphs fully by asking the questions a professional writer might ask—"Does the paragraph stick to one point? Do the sentences flow logically and smoothly? Have I given the reader enough information? Do the listeners understand what I mean? Does the group have any questions about my paragraph? How can I make it clearer?"

Read your thesis statement, conclusion, and guiding sentences out loud to the group. Ask, "Are all related?"

Listen to the responses.

Discuss ways of changing or improving paragraphs, sentences, or sequences of ideas.

Share and discuss your collections of opening and closing paragraphs from published articles.

APPLICATION

During Lectures, In Class: Listen for guiding ideas. You will recognize a guiding idea when the speaker begins a new topic. You will know that supporting details or idea expanders will follow. You will *hear* paragraph changes and will not feel that you must take down every word a speaker utters.

For your next lecture class, divide a notebook page into two columns, or fold the page in half. Label the first column *Guiding Ideas;* label the second column *Idea Expanders.* When the speaker announces a broad topic, write the topic across the page, spanning both columns. The first broad topic might be the title of the lecture. As you listen to the speaker, place guiding ideas in column one, followed by idea expanders in column two. You will notice that the number of idea expanders differs with each topic, each speaker, and indeed, with each paragraph.

After class, as soon as possible, meet with another student or a small group and compare notes.

While Studying: Examine three or four paragraphs from the chapter you are reading to determine the guiding idea in each. Test the guiding idea by asking, "What does the author say about the guiding idea in the guiding sentence? How does each of the other sentences expand upon the guiding idea?'' This exercise will reveal whether your textbook's paragraphs are written as clearly as those in the Farb essay. They may be as well-organized, but, you cannot depend on it. However, you may see a pattern emerging which will help you understand the author's organization. Knowing the author's pattern of organization will increase your understanding of the text.

Underline or highlight only guiding sentences in paragraphs as you read a chapter assignment. Do not underline the author's examples, illustrations, or idea expanders unless you do not fully understand their purposes or they include new or technical information which you must memorize. In cases where you wish to highlight supporting details, use a different color highlighter, or a pencil and ruler, to clearly distinguish supporting information from guiding ideas.

Outlining will become more useful if you use the textbook's headings as major divisions. For example, in your outline, use the Roman numerals *I, II, III*, etc., for the largest headings in the chapter. Use the guiding idea of each paragraph as subdivisions *A, B, C*, etc. Include the important supporting details or idea expanders in the outline as numbers *1, 2, 3*, etc., under the appropriate guiding idea. Experiment with different ways of outlining to see which you prefer. You may use a full sentence outline, a phrase outline, or a word outline. Whichever you choose, make certain that later, when you reread the outline, long after it is written, you are still able to understand it.

Taking essay examinations will produce less anxiety when you apply your knowledge of paragraph construction to answering essay questions. For example, turning the essay question into a statement may give you either a thesis for your answer or a guiding idea. In your response to an essay question, think about paragraph development and stick to the question. Essay examinations will be discussed fully in a later chapter.

six

Re-Reading/Writing: Critical Thinking

How are you doing? How does it feel to have completed a first draft? Getting a first draft on paper is not a simple task; it is quite an accomplishment. It takes both concentration and craft. However, it is only the beginning of a writer's work. In phases one and two, you approached the craft of writing as professional writers do, both systematically and creatively. In phase three, you will reread and rewrite, reinvent, reorder, and revise until your product pleases you. Just as an artist refines and adds details to a painting, you will return, again and again, to your canvas of words for *re-vision*, or seeing again, but, each time from a different perspective.

First, to effectively prepare for this chapter, a progress review is in order to determine what you have accomplished and learned in the preceding chapters. Take a few moments now to free write in answer to the following *Progress Review Questions*:

How have your daily reading and writing practices changed since you began this book? Have you been keeping up with daily journal writing and pleasure reading? Are you monitoring your reading habits and writing processes? Where have you made the most progress? In which areas do you need more practice? How close are you to becoming an independent learner? Look through the table of contents of this text; which chapters need rereading? How are you doing in your other courses? What can you take from this book to improve your understanding and responses to other academic subjects? How can you move beyond this text to even more creative ways of learning?

In writing the first draft for "A Meaningful Period," what were some of your personal writing behaviors? How did you choose to approach the writing task? How much time had you spent thinking about your topic before writing? How much advance information (notes) had you accumulated before you started writing? How much time did you spend on the first draft? Did you spend any time revising or changing the draft? When did you make these changes? Did you make changes after the draft was written or as you were writing? What did you do when revising? List the revision strategies you used. About how much time did you spend rewriting your first draft?

Get into the habit of checking your progress in other areas of your life as well by asking, Where are my greatest strengths? Where are my weaknesses? How can I use my strengths to improve my weaknesses? What are my primary goals and priorities? What area of priority must I concentrate on first? When I see progress in my first goal, what are my second, third, and fourth goals? Use free writing and your journals for regular progress reviews and do not hesitate to rearrange your priorities when necessary. You are in charge of your priorities, progress, and growth. Please take your progress review seriously, because you are about to embark on a crucial phase in your growth as reader, writer, and learner.

WHAT YOU CAN EXPECT
FROM THIS CHAPTER

In Chapter Six, a key concept will emerge clearly—the concept that *rereading* is the key to both the revision of what you write and the understanding of what you read. When you reread for revision or understanding, you will be practicing the *critical thinking* skills of observation, judgment, and evaluation. As reader/writer, you will reread all or portions of a text (your own or another author's) with specific critical purposes in mind; you will not reread randomly.

As a careful and critical writer, you will reread your original drafts for purpose, meaning, and organization. You will learn how to test your writing for its content, shape, order, and flow. Checklists will provide guidelines which may be used for all your writing projects. When necessary, you will use a writing handbook to check for mechanical errors in grammar, punctuation, and spelling.

As a careful and critical reader, you will reread another author's text with the same awareness that you bring to your own writing. Checklists will provide the clues you need for getting more meaning from everything you read. You will find that the combination of purposeful reading and a writer's perspective will increase your comprehension and retention of information.

DELIBERATE READING AND FORMAL WRITING

Deliberate reading is the reading rate used for rereading and rethinking about text. It is slower than the moderate speed used for examining details. It allows you to stop and weigh ideas, to ponder, change, take notes, and rewrite. Deliberate reading is performed with care and without haste. You will use deliberate reading each time you revise your own writing or reread another author's work.

Formal writing is a way of shaping or *forming* a first draft into an organized whole. The shape of the writing is determined by its nature. For example, an essay's shape and form is different from the shape of a textbook chapter or term paper. Because formal writing is a result of the re-reading/writing process, it is accomplished at a slower pace than focused writing.

Formal writing and deliberate reading are complementary processes. Formal writing enables you to formalize or shape-up a rough draft through deliberate reading; deliberate reading helps you to see how other authors have formed or shaped their work. Both formal writing and deliberate reading are essential to the process of re-reading/writing. Unfortunately, inexperienced readers/writers frequently omit the re-reading/writing phase, erroneously believing that the first and only reading of a text is sufficient, or that they are finished with a draft the moment the last word is written. As readers, they unrealistically expect to remember important facts after a single reading. As writers, they seem to believe that their first draft is engraved in stone—they are that reluctant to change or alter their prose.

The truth is, the inexperienced writer/reader is stumped. He or she has not the foggiest notion of how to change, alter, or revise a first draft. Time limitations in school situations have prevented revision from being given the same serious attention that professional writers have been giving it all along. In one semester it is impossible to learn what the professional writer has taken a lifetime to discover. On the other hand, if you, as a student, are taught early about how writers reread and revise, you will progress faster as an independent learner, and this knowledge will shorten significantly the trial and error period that all readers, writers, and learners experience. Finally, it is essential that you understand that rewriting is both the expression of craft and of creativity. For while you are rereading, reformulating, and revising, you are indeed *recreating* as well. For many writers, *Re-viewing* or *seeing again* is the most creative stage of all.

THE POWER OF RE-VIEWING

Both the reading and writing of an essay or chapter may be compared to building a house. A builder visualizes the overall design from basement to roof, then draws a diagram to show how the house will look. (The process is similar to free writing or skimming for thesis, conclusion, and smaller, related ideas.) However, the house remains an empty shell until it is subdivided into separate rooms, each of which is sketched individually. (The process is similar to reading for details or writing paragraphs of a first draft.) Before the builder can put the finishing touches on the house, the following questions must be answered about the rooms:

What is each room's purpose?

How does each room achieve its purpose?

Does each room have an orderly design?

Is the arrangement of rooms best for the overall design of the house?

Is the flow of traffic from one room to another smooth and clear?

Do the rooms achieve their individual purposes, yet work together for a smooth flow of traffic?

As a house does, an essay or chapter requires a review of the original plan or design before the project can be completed. The builder's rooms may be compared to paragraphs in an essay or chapter. Paragraphs, like rooms, must have purpose. Each must have its own plan yet fit in with the other units and the overall design. Each must flow smoothly from the preceding paragraph and into the following one. As a builder *reviews* each room before completing a house, similarly, the reader/writer *re-views* each paragraph before completing an essay, or before fully comprehending another author's meaning. Therefore, the builder's review may be compared with the reader/writer's *re-view*.

RE-VIEWING THE PARAGRAPH

In the rereading/writing phase, you will be inspecting closely each paragraph of your first draft. However, do not be put off by the prefix *re* in re-viewing and rereading/writing. Although *re* means *again*, and implies returning or going back, you will not be doing the same thing more than once. Instead, re-viewing suggests that you are *looking* for something *new* and different each time you revisit a portion of text. Moreover, what you *see* through re-reading/writing may surprise and excite you.

Looking For
Paragraph Purpose

A paragraph has purpose when its guiding sentence is related to the essay's thesis, and when all other sentences expand upon the guiding idea. *As a reader*, you will find purposeful paragraphs easy to skim. *As a writer*, do not include a paragraph in your final draft until you give it a purpose. If you cannot decide what a particular paragraph's purpose is, more thought and planning may be needed. Generally, the purpose of a paragraph is to expand, extend, or explain the guiding idea of the guiding sentence.

A paragraph without a purpose is like a daisy growing in a tomato patch; it may be lovely to look at, but it won't go well with bacon and lettuce on toast. And so it is with a paragraph. You must know how it will fit in with the goals and purposes of the whole essay or term paper that you are writing.

Looking For
Paragraph Order

The order or sequence of sentences in a paragraph is closely linked to purpose. If the sentences that expand upon the guiding idea are thrown together randomly, without logic or order, the paragraph cannot achieve its purpose, nor will it be clear to the reader. The sequence of sentences in a paragraph depends on the nature of the subject.

For descriptions of persons, places, or things, *visual* or *spatial* order is used. For example, you might visually describe a person from head to toe, or a place spatially from left to right, or from bottom to top. Extended explanations of processes or events require *chronological* order. Most general subjects use *order of increasing importance* to enhance the reader's understanding and to heighten interest.

Visual, or *Spatial Order* abounds in fiction, yet writers of factual information frequently use fictional devices to enliven their prose. The following paragraph uses both spatial and visual order:

> Between class periods, college students move across the campus from an ivy-covered building to an ultramodern hall, shifting subjects and changing frames of mind. In one classroom, students enter quietly, take sheets of white, ruled paper from the flat desk at the front of the room, return to their seats and begin to write. The class period starts officially without fanfare or announcement, and once in a while the instructor looks up at the large, round clock on the wall.

Did you notice how the writer takes the reader from place to place in a smooth, logical progression? First, outside on a college campus, then inside a classroom, and second, from the front of the room to the classroom seats. The plan for visual or spatial order is logic. As the writer, use your mind as a camera's eye to *pan* or move through a scene smoothly. As you write, ask yourself, "What must I know about my subject in order to *show* the reader? As the reader, what would I need to *see* first? What is the best way of ordering the remaining ideas so that the reader will understand what I mean?" Use visual or spatial order whenever you want to *show* rather than *tell* your reader something.

Chronological Order is used when your subject demands a time sequence. For instance, if you are describing an event, list the related happenings in the order in which they naturally occur: the crowd gathered in the stadium; the teams appeared on the field; the game started at three p.m.; at the end of the ninth inning, the score was tied; the game ran twelve innings; the stadium did not empty out until after dark.

If the first fact, *the crowd gathered in the stadium*, had been wrongly placed in the paragraph, the reader would be thrown off balance and might not continue to read. Remember, the writer's job is to make the reader's job easier. Notice the clear, chronological paragraph pattern in the next paragraph.

> If subjects are awakened during their first REM period, they recall a dream about 60 percent of the time; if awakened during the second REM period, the recall level rises to 70 percent; for subsequent REM periods, the recall rate remains about 85 percent. As the night progresses, the dream reports tend to become increasingly long, vivid, and emotional. References to electrodes, the EEG machine, the experimenter, or other aspects of the laboratory setting often are incorporated into the dreams, particularly during the first few nights of sleeping in the novel laboratory situation. Waking preoccupations, such as an interest in sports, singing, or cars, may be reflected in more than one dream of a night, but no obvious linkages exist among the various dreams from a single night in terms of story plot or developing theme. A later dream does not begin where an earlier one left off.[1]

Order of Increasing Importance is used in most general paragraphs to maintain the reader's attention and to build interest in the subject. As a reader, if you discover that a writer places the most interesting information in the first sentence of every paragraph, you might decide to skim the work instead of wasting time on less important or less interesting details. You would quickly lose patience with an essay or chapter that let you down at the end of every paragraph. As a reader, you expect the writer to keep up the subject's momentum, to hold your attention, and to continue to build your interest throughout the piece.

[1]From *Humankind* by Peter Farb. Copyright © 1978 by Peter Farb. Reprinted by permission of Houghton Mifflin Company and Jonathan Cape Limited.

On the other hand, if your purpose for reading is to get the central facts, you would indeed choose to skim, or you would turn to a newspaper where all the important questions are answered in the lead. The newspaper reporter tells *Who, What, Where, When,* and *How* immediately, while other writers draw the reader into the subject gradually.

An example of order of increasing importance can be seen in the final paragraph of Farb's essay.

> REM sleep, in contrast, apparently restores the neural processes underlying consciousness; it is mental rather than physical. People deprived of it are not physically lethargic but emotionally irritable; they usually perform poorly in concentration and learning tests. REM sleep appears to be essential to integrate recently learned material into long-term memory. Students who stay up all night cramming for an examination the next day usually do not do as well as those who have had some sleep. The explanation is that the students have momentarily learned a lot of new facts, but these facts cannot be remembered unless they have been processed during sleep for incorporation into the memory. REM sleep also seems to help people cope with day-to-day stress. Experiments have shown that volunteers who were exposed to stressful situations had a sharply increased need for REM sleep, during which time they apparently made peace with the traumatic experiences. Such experiments offer fresh evidence that sleep is one of the most active parts of a person's day.[2]

To summarize, sentences in a paragraph may be written in spatial or visual order, chronological order, or in the order of increasing importance. As a reader, a growing familiarity with order, or logical sequencing of ideas, will enhance your understanding of textual material. As a writer, familiarity with your subject will suggest the best order of sentences and paragraphs. However, even the most practiced writers may not see the best sequence immediately. More often, knowledge of the appropriate order may not become fully evident until many words have been written, many ideas reformulated, and many sentences and paragraphs reordered.

Looking For Transitions

Transitions are word bridges built by writers to carry readers over gaps between ideas. Gaps may occur anywhere in a written text. Our use of punctuation, the period in particular, fosters the need for transitions: A sentence contains a single thought. Period. The next sentence begins. Period. A paragraph expands upon a single idea. Period. The next paragraph begins.

Reading would be a jarring experience if not for transitions.

[2]From *Humankind* by Peter Farb. Copyright © 1978 by Peter Farb. Reprinted by permission of Houghton Mifflin Company and Jonathan Cape Limited.

Transitional words or phrases lead the reader smoothly from idea to idea, holding the attention, avoiding the distraction of a sentence coming to an end, or a paragraph coming to a close. Without transitions, a paragraph is difficult to read, an essay is choppy, a chapter is a series of abrupt stops and starts. Most readers, lured by a smooth flow of words, are not consciously aware of transitions. On the other hand, a reader can immediately sense the absence of transitional devices.

Most transitions have one major purpose—to pick up something recognizable from one idea, sentence, or paragraph, and to carry it forward to the next—very much like a link in a chain. This carryover is achieved by repeating a word, phrase, or idea or through the use of specific transitional words or groups of words. A secondary purpose of transitions, other than connecting ideas, is to give directional and predictive clues to the reader. In other words, transitions signal the reader about where the writing is going. For example, the phrase, *on the other hand*, tells the reader that a contrasting or different idea will follow while the phrase, *for example*, signals the reader to expect an illustration or example that will explain a concept already mentioned.

As a reader, your increasing awareness of transitions will help you predict as you read. The ability to predict what comes next is a characteristic of efficient readers. As a writer, your increasing use of transitions will result in clearer prose. The facility with many appropriate transitions is a sign of a competent writer. As a speaker, you use transitions all the time. Listen for them, and learn to use them in your writing. The following is a list of transactions used frequently in speech and text:

and	even so	therefore
also	furthermore	though
but	for instance	too
besides	instead	yet

As a reader, you have already experienced the value of effective and smooth transitions in a text. As a writer, it is your obligation to provide these same transitions between ideas for the reader of your work. If the writing of transitions is left to chance, many writers, including myself, tend to rely on a few favorites. As a result, the writing is less lively. A professor once remarked that a mediocre piece of writing could be improved immeasurably simply by adding interesting and varied transitions. The professor may have exaggerated a bit, but she nevertheless spoke from a background of knowledge, both of student writing and professional writing. The professor recommended collecting transitions and keeping them near the typewriter. Here are some to start your collection.

TRANSITIONAL WORDS AND PHRASES THAT SIGNAL THE ADDITION OF MORE INFORMATION

also	as proof	for this reason
an example of	besides	furthermore
another	for example	in addition
as an illustration	for instance	that is

TRANSITIONAL WORDS AND PHRASES THAT SIGNAL COMPARISON: TO SHOW LIKENESS OR SIMILARITY

also	in a similar way	similarly
besides	in the same way	therefore
furthermore	likewise	thus
in a like manner	moreover	too

TRANSITIONAL WORDS AND PHRASES THAT SIGNAL CONTRAST: TO SHOW DIFFERENCE OR DIRECTIONAL CHANGE

although	in spite of	other
but	instead	otherwise
conversely	nevertheless	still
despite	nonetheless	though
even so	notwithstanding	while
even though	on the contrary	yet
however	on the other hand	
in contrast	or	

TRANSITIONAL WORDS AND PHRASES THAT SHOW A CAUSE AND EFFECT RELATIONSHIP

accordingly	consequently	since
as a result	hence	so
because	therefore	
because of this	thus	

TRANSITIONAL WORDS AND PHRASES THAT SHOW SEQUENCE OR CHRONOLOGY

after	during	not long after
after that	finally	one, two
afterward	first, second	once, now
as soon as	finally	shortly
at first	following	soon
at last	frequently	then
at length	in the first place	the next
at the same time	later	thereafter
at the outset	later on	to begin with
before	meanwhile	when
before long	next	while

TRANSITIONAL WORDS AND PHRASES THAT SUMMARIZE

accordingly	consequently	in short
all in all	finally	that is
as a result	for this reason	therefore
as I have shown	in conclusion	thus
as you can see	in other words	

To summarize, transitions, which may be called the glue or cement that keeps ideas together, are essential to the clear understanding of a text. Good readers recognize effective transitions and use them to *predict* what may come next. Good writers collect transitions and use them in their writing to help the reader become a better predictor, and to give their writing *cohesion*, a smooth, flowing quality. In short, transitions are needed by reader, writer, and speaker to bridge the gaps between ideas, sentences, and paragraphs. But most important, the effective use of transitions enables reader, writer, and speaker to communicate more clearly.

RE-VIEWING THE FIRST DRAFT

Rereading what you have written is the only way to revise. However, you cannot expect to reread a draft once and revise it to your satisfaction. As the author, you will have to reread your work a number of times. Reading randomly may work for some writers, but *planned* re-reading/ writing is more effective. With planned re-reading/writing, the reader/writer goes over the work a number of times, but each time for *one* specific purpose. In this way, the predetermined item which the reader/writer has chosen to look for, tends to "pop out" as he or she re-reads/writes. You may choose to re-read/write any number of times, but if you are facing a deadline or due date, three times should be enough. At the first reading, look at *Meaning*; at the second, look for *Meandering*; at the third reading, look at *Mechanics*.

Looking At Meaning

To look at meaning in your first draft, you will ask of the whole piece, "Does it make sense? Is it clear and understandable? Do ideas flow logically? Is it interesting?" Having been immersed in the material from its inception, however, may make the questions difficult to answer. As the writer, you will tend to look at your material *subjectively*, from the inside. In re-reading/writing, you will have to act as a reader, looking at your material *objectively*, from the outside. To alter your perspective from subjective to objective and to better answer the questions about meaning, you will have to change the form of your material.

Changing the form of your material is not difficult; it is in fact enjoyable for most students and provides just enough diversion and variety at a time when your concentration is intensifying. Basically, if you have been writing in longhand, you can change your draft's form by *hearing* what is sounds like and *seeing* what it looks like in print. In other words, reading it aloud and typing it will change the perspective.

Because you are experienced as a speaker and listener, reading your draft aloud will enable you to *hear* some of your errors in writing even as you utter the words. If you stumble over a sentence, perhaps the writing is not smooth. As you read from your text, you may hear what you did not at first see. You may notice that although you are *saying* a word correctly, it is *written* differently, and therefore its spelling must be verified. As you read aloud, mark in pencil the areas to be revised or verified. Tape your reading. You may hear more clearly when you are not *both* speaking and looking at the text. Better yet, find a "live" audience. Try it out on a friend and in return offer to listen to your friend's paper or report. But before reading to another person, tell that person specifically what you want to know about your work. Ask your listener, "Do you hear a beginning, middle, and ending? Do you hear a *This is what I am going to say* statement? Where in the text is it? Do you hear a *This is what I have said* statement? Where in the text is it? Is any portion of the draft not clear, not understandable, not consistent or logical?" Remind your friend that, as your audience, he or she may learn something important about communication skills as well as something about friendship.

After reading aloud and revising the draft, type a clean copy. Seeing your work in print can be enlightening. Errors you may have missed in longhand or may not have heard in reading, will stand out on the printed page. If you had composed the first draft on a typewriter, rather than in longhand, a freshly typed copy can have a similar effect.

Looking For Meandering

To meander is to wind and turn from a predetermined course or direction. In writing, going "off the track," digressing, or not "sticking to the point" can be called meandering. Meandering should not be confused with the winding and turning of the writing process itself. Writers move in and out, backward and forward, or in circular fashion while in the *process* of writing, precisely to keep the *product* on an orderly course. Writers are keenly aware that the product, or text, may have purpose and direction if it is to be understood. Use a freshly typed copy of your draft to check for meandering and "track" your topic with color.

Tracking Your Topic
With Color

To look for meandering, ask, "Does the work have shape, order, logic, flow?" In other words, is it well-organized? To track your work's organization, you have to do something that brings out, or highlights, the skeleton, or structure. One way of highlighting the structure is to use different colored marking pens, crayons, or highlighters on your copy. The principle of highlighting the skeleton of your written work is similar to an x-ray technician injecting colored dyes into the body's veins when checking for physical ailments. Therefore, to cure a broad spectrum of structural ailments in your writing, and to help you *visualize* the shape of your work, put your draft on the x-ray table.

First, find your thesis statement and highlight it; pick any instrument and any color that pleases you. (If you use a highlighter, run it through the text; if you use pens, take a ruler and underline the appropriate portions of text. Feel free to use a combination of highlighters, pens, or crayons.) Then read your concluding statement and highlight it in the *same* color *only if it clearly ties in with the thesis.* If it doesn't tie in, rewrite it until it does, then highlight.

Second, locate all of the smaller, related ideas that are now in guiding sentences, and give *each* idea a *different* identifying color. Highlight or underline the guiding sentence in each of the *middle* paragraphs *only if the guiding sentence clearly ties in with the thesis.* If it doesn't tie in, rewrite it until it does, then highlight. Next, check the supporting details in each paragraph and, *if they tie in with the guiding sentence,* highlight them in the same color as the guiding idea. Finally, check for smooth transitions by reading the last sentence of a paragraph and the first sentence of the paragraph that follows it. Use a single color for transitions and highlight the last and first sentences of adjacent paragraphs *if you see and hear the transition between them.* If not, create the transition, then highlight. Transitional sentences that work will have two colors; the first matches the guiding idea, and the second is the color reserved for transitions.

Look at your colorful writing. What do you see? Are there any bare areas, portions of text not highlighted? Read them. Why were they not highlighted? Lack of color may signify sections not related to the thesis or may, in their bareness, highlight transitional sentences, sentences used for transitions from one sentence to another. If they are transitional sentences, color them with the transition tone, then reexamine the other untinted areas. You may delete, move, replace, or reorder these portions of text. Some portions may be more closely related to other guiding ideas and may better fit into other paragraphs. On the other hand, some unhighlighted text may contain *new,* related ideas which can be developed into new paragraphs. Decide where they best fit. You may have to write, or rewrite transitions. At this point, you can regroup, reorder, or rearrange ideas that were once meandering. Most important, you will know that your topic is on the right track.

Looking At Mechanics

After you have reread and rewritten your work for meaning and for meandering, you are ready to check the mechanics. Looking at a draft for the mechanics of grammar, punctuation, and spelling is a personal matter, with each individual developing his or her own system. The system you use for checking the mechanics of your work should be based on your particular problems or oversights in each of the three areas. If you have never had a spelling problem, there is no reason to check your work for spelling; chances are a misspelled word will stand out as you are reading for other purposes. On the other hand, if you frequently use pronouns incorrectly, it would be wise to read the draft at least once, specifically for inspecting pronoun usage. The same holds true for punctuation. Now, you may be thinking, "Suppose I am not able to identify my grammar, punctuation, or spelling problems, then what do I do?"

If, at this time, you do not have a clear sense of judgment of the mechanics of writing, there are a number of ways you may proceed. First, you can do the best you can with your paper by typing a clean draft, then having someone else look at the mechanics. You may have a friend or parent who will do this for you, or you can take your finished work to the school's learning center or writing lab. Second, you may wish to hand the paper in with a *self-evaluation* which would enable your instructor to advise you further. Once you see where your paper needs further work in mechanics, you can better judge future writing projects. Keep a writing handbook near your work area to use as a reference tool and to review concepts once learned but perhaps forgotten. The third option, is to use the *Mechanics Checklist* on page 125, preferably in conjunction with a handbook and with your first graded paper. The *Mechanics Checklist* addresses some of the most common writing errors.

SUMMARY

Re-reading/writing, the third phase in the reading/writing process, can be both inventive and creative. Planned and practiced *re-viewing* is a powerful technique. It may be used for clarifying the meaning of any textual material. Checking for meandering keeps "writing in progress" on a desired course. An inspection of mechanics clears errors in grammar, punctuation, and spelling. Moreover, many of the same techniques you use to improve an original draft can be used to extract more meaning from another writer's work.

GETTING THE PICTURE

The Paragraph

A diagram of a paragraph might look like a flower with the guiding idea as its center and related sentences growing out of the center like petals, as shown in Figure 6-1.

Paragraphs In A Chapter
Or Essay

Although each paragraph is an individual unit of an essay or chapter, it is connected to the central idea or thesis, and is linked to the paragraphs which precede and follow it. A diagram of an essay or chapter showing relationships among paragraphs might look like a chain. See Figure 6-2.

PARAGRAPH CHECKLIST

READER'S QUESTIONS	WRITER'S QUESTIONS
	Purpose
Is the purpose of each of the author's paragraphs evident?	What is the purpose of each of my paragraphs?
Does each paragraph achieve its purpose?	Does each of my paragraphs achieve its purpose?

How can the purpose of each paragraph be improved?

FIGURE 6-1
The Paragraph

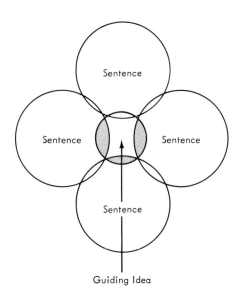

Guiding Idea

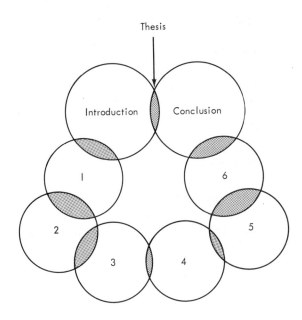

FIGURE 6-2
Paragraphs Linked Together
in an Essay or Chapter

Order

Are the sentences in each paragraph arranged logically? Is there enough information, or do I have unanswered questions?

What is the best arrangement of sentences in each paragraph? Does each of my paragraphs contain enough information for the reader?

How can the order of sentences in a paragraph be improved?

TRANSITIONS

Does each sentence flow smoothly and naturally to the next one?

Does each sentence flow smoothly and naturally to the next one?

Does each paragraph flow smoothly and naturally to the next one?

Does each paragraph flow smoothly and naturally to the next one?

How can the flow, through the use of transitions, be improved?

CHECKLIST FOR MEANING

Does the chapter or essay have a beginning, middle, and ending? Is there a thesis statement or a *This is what I am going to say* statement?

Is there a concluding, summarizing, or *This is what I have said* statement?

CHECKLIST FOR AVOIDING MEANDERING

Does each paragraph have a guiding idea?

Is the guiding idea related to the thesis?

Is the guiding idea expressed in the guiding sentence?

Do all the paragraph's sentences expand upon the guiding idea?

Are each of the paragraph's guiding ideas related to the thesis?

Are each of the paragraph's guiding ideas related to one another?

Is there a relationship among thesis, conclusion, and guiding ideas?

MECHANICS CHECKLIST

(To be used in conjunction with a writing handbook)

Does each sentence have a subject and verb?

Is there agreement between subject and verb in each sentence?

Are pronouns used correctly?

Is there agreement between pronoun and verb in each sentence?

Are adverbs and adjectives used correctly?

Has misuse of punctuation been corrected?

Have misspellings been corrected?

REVISION CHECKLIST

Delete useless information.

Cross out words that merely occupy space.

Use one word instead of two or three, wherever possible.

Replace difficult words with more common words.

Divide long sentences into shorter statements (as long as each statement has both a subject and a verb).

Change negative statements to positive ones, if possible.

Make general statements more specific.

Subsitute another word for "very."

Use the words "a lot" and "all right" instead of the incorrect single-word spellings.

INDEPENDENT ACTIVITIES

I. *PROGRESS REVIEW*

Read from beginning to end the rewritten draft of "A Meaningful Period."

Reflect on the following questions.

Write a few words in answer to each question.

    a. Did the re-reading/writing approach I used work for me? Why? Why not? If not, how can I approach the task differently next time?

    b. How long had I thought about my topic before revising the first draft?

    c. How much additional information (notes) had I accumulated before starting the actual rewriting?

    d. How much time did I spend on the revision?

        1. What are the strengths of this revised version? Place a check mark next to the portion you believe to be well done.

        2. What are the weaknesses of this revised version? Place an *X* next to the portion you believe can be improved.

        3. How much revision remains to be done?

        4. How will I go about improving the revised draft? Make a list of strategies you might use to improve the piece.

II. *Read* the material on *Sleep* in the appendix.

    Reflect on the thesis statement, "All human beings share the need for sleep, yet individual sleep patterns are varied; and it has been said that one's personality may be related to the number of hours one sleeps each night." Using this thesis statement, *Write* an essay on sleep in which you classify the general population into the following four sleep groups:

    a. Those who sleep four or fewer hours a night.

    b. Those who sleep six hours a night.

    c. Those who sleep eight hours a night.

    d. Those who sleep ten or more hours a night.

The purpose of the assignment is to enable you to concentrate on your writing skills and to think less about organization. It is however, creative, because you will have to be convincing.

Include the following:

    1. Give the essay an original title.

    2. Develop and describe a hypothetical personality type for each sleep category.

3. Quote from the appendix material (on the subject of sleep) to support your descriptions and characteristics.

Introduction

In your introduction, build up to the thesis statement by using one of the following methods for beginning your essay.

a. Tell why the topic is important or of interest to the reader.
b. Give some background information on the subject (this may be quoted or paraphrased from the appendix material or from another source).
c. Ask a question.
d. Use a pertinent quotation.
e. Tell an incident, brief story, or anecdote that sets the stage for the thesis statement.

Middle Paragraphs

Discuss each of the personality types in one or more paragraphs:

a. Give a description or characteristics of the type.
b. Include supporting details: Why is the person like this? How did the person get this way?
c. Show the relationship between the person's personality and his or her sleep pattern.

Conclusion

Convince your reader that you have accomplished what you have set out to do by summarizing, by restating the thesis, or by offering one new fact that ties everything together.

a. Check your draft against the *Paragraph Checklist, Checklist for Meaning, Checklist to Avoid Meandering, Mechanics Checklist*, and *Revision Checklist*.
b. NOTE: Although you will have to make inferences about people who sleep a certain number of hours each night, and you will have to come to some logical, supported conclusions about their personality types, *there are no right or wrong personality types*. But, you must be convincing.

III. Assay the selection, "Dealing With Troubled Sleep" (page 148), by highlighting or underlining, in color, the thesis, conclusion, and guiding sentences.

GROUP ACTIVITIES

Share one or more selected portions of your *Progress Review* with the class or a small group.

Listen to others' comments on the *Progress Review*.

Discuss the nature of the comments.

Compare the comments of the group.

What generalization can you make about the reading and writing behaviors of the group?

Share your personal re-reading/writing experiences with the group. Which methods worked best for you?

Listen to others' comments on re-reading/writing. Are there methods which worked for others that you may try on your next writing project?

Discuss further the methods that seemed to work best for most of the group's members.

What conclusion can you draw about re-reading/writing?

Discuss with the group your plans for writing the essay on sleep in which you are given the thesis statement.

Compare plans for the *introduction*. How many students found interesting samples of "openings" of published articles? What sort of "introduction" is popular at the present time?

Collect (from the group) the three best models of opening paragraphs and share them with the class.

Discuss the assay of the selection, "Dealing With Troubled Sleep."

APPLICATION

During Lectures, In Class: Listen for "openings" in lectures and class lessons. What can you predict about a lecture from the introduction?

Listen for "closings." Can you hear the concluding statement?

Listen for meandering. Are there speakers who tend to meander or digress from their subject? When does this occur? How do they manage to get back to the subject—or do they?

What can you learn about public speaking from listening?

While Studying: Examine openings and closings in your textbook chapters.

Mark those that are outstanding.

When Taking Examinations: Listen for openings, closings, and meandering (if any) in the directions given by the test administrator. Is the level of meandering lower when the speaker gives directions? If so, why? What can you conclude about the differences (or sameness) of lectures, class talks, and direction-giving for examinations?

What generalizations can you make about purpose, order (or sequence), and transitions in speech, lectures, and verbal directions?

seven

Using Techniques Taught

If you have read carefully Chapters One through Six, have completed independent and group activities, and have applied techniques taught, you are prepared for this chapter. Chapter Seven shows how everything you have learned thus far can be applied to the essay examination and the research paper. More important, applications are not limited to tests and papers but apply as well to business reports and other important communications, letters, and memos. If you have come this far in *Read, Reflect, Write*, you are well on your way to becoming an Independent Learner. Do not be discouraged, however, if writing projects or reading tasks still present challenges; they will continue to do so. However, as you grow in reading/writing competencies, you will welcome each new challenge.

WHAT YOU CAN EXPECT
FROM THIS CHAPTER

In Chapter Seven you will see how knowledge of beginnings, middles, endings, paragraph construction, and the three phases of reading/writing work together to prepare you for writing a research paper and taking an essay examination. As you worked through this book, you have indeed experienced some of the methods that will be mentioned again. However, what is most valuable about Chapter Seven is that it will show you how to make use of what you already *know* to tackle the new and *unknown*.

Uppermost in the mind of an Independent Learner, as he or she continues to gain knowledge, is the question, "How can I apply elsewhere this recently acquired information?" Some of you have already asked that question—and perhaps answered it as well. But, for *application* to continue to work in your learning life, you must constantly seek out and search for, with a magnifying glass at times, connections and relationships among concepts and things. Each time you read a passage, write and revise, alter and substitute, add and delete, you make new connections and combinations. Even the task of re-reading/writing for the purpose of revision is a creative act, an inventive review, and applying the known to the unknown is an exciting strand of creativity. That is why the application of familiar *Read, Reflect, Write* techniques to a crucial area such as the essay examination should indeed inspire confidence and make test taking less stressful. When you follow the test-taking method that follows, you will find, on your very next examination, that you have more time and energy to concentrate on effectively answering the questions, rather than worrying about answering correctly or not having enough time to complete the exam.

TAKING ESSAY EXAMINATIONS

Studies clearly have shown that the most common cause of error on written essay examinations is *not understanding the question*. Other common errors include not being specific (making too many generalizations), writing long, rambling, disorganized answers, not proofreading to eliminate careless mistakes, and failing to use the allotted test time wisely. To assure yourself an optimal chance of success on your next essay examination, consider each one of these errors, but concentrate on correcting those that have given you trouble in the past.

To correct each of the five areas of potential error, you must ask the following questions *before* each examination: "Do I clearly understand the questions? How can I best budget the time allotted for this test?" *During* the test, ask, "What is the best organization (of ideas) for my response to this question?" *After* responding to all of the questions, ask, "Have I clearly written my answers? Have I proofread and corrected each answer?"

Understanding the Question:

It is most important that you quickly read the entire test from start to finish before you begin to work. This is similar to the skimming or pre-reading technique in that it gives you an overview and you immediately know what is expected of you. It is different from skimming in that you will *read the test with your pencil.* Marking key portions of the questions and jotting down first thoughts about answers will prevent you from mis-reading or overlooking parts of questions.

First, circle the key words in the question. Key words are directives such as *define, describe, discuss, explain, list.* Other key words may include numbers. For example, you may be asked to give three examples, two illustrations, or four causes of a particular event. Marking key words highlights the essential points in the directions and prevents you from losing points on the test through oversight.

Second, number the separate parts of the question. Many essays are made up of two, three, or four segments. Numbering prevents you from omitting any of the segments.

Third, as you are reading the question, jot down those first important impressions of answers as they occur to you. Do this in the margins right next to the question, or on scrap paper if you cannot write in the test booklet. By doing this, you relieve your mind of trying to recall those first thoughts later. Also your jottings will start a chain of associations about the topic in question.

Fourth, check carefully to see how many questions you are required to answer. If you are asked to answer only three out of four, put an *X* through the question that is most difficult for you. It is not unusual for a student to overlook this option; he or she attempts to complete all questions, then finds there is not enough time to complete the last part of the test, nor is there time to proofread and verify answers.

Budgeting the Allotted Time for the Test:

After you have determined how many questions you are required to answer, jot down a plan to make full use of the time allowed. For example, if you are asked to answer four essay questions and you have two hours in which to complete the examination, divide the time into four segments, allowing twenty-five minutes for each question and the extra twenty minutes for prereading and proofreading. Write down the starting and stopping time for each question, and remember to look at the clock periodically. If the test questions carry different point values, be sure to allot more time, proportionately, for answering questions with heavier point value. When you budget your test time, you prevent yourself from spending too much time on the first few questions and racing frantically through the final ones.

Organizing Ideas Before Writing
the Answer to the Question:

Here is where your *Read, Reflect, Write* experience will come in most handy. An answer to an essay question, if it is to be organized, will have a beginning, middle, and ending.

It is a good idea to outline each answer before putting it into essay form. An effective *beginning* is simply a restatement of the question. In other words, you turn the question into a guiding idea which becomes the guiding sentence. By doing this, you reinforce the question in your mind, you stay on the topic, you avoid meandering, and you state *this is what I am going to say*. The *middle* portion of the answer is where you add specific details to support the guiding sentence. Specific details include names, dates, examples, and illustrations. Details may also include comparisons, contrasts, exceptions, implications—depending, of course, upon the key words that you underlined or highlighted in the question. The middle portion of the answer is where you *say it*. The ending, *this is what I have said*, may summarize the information you have included, or it may be a restatement, in different words, of your guiding idea. By outlining first, you get the skeleton of an answer on paper; then if you run out of time later, you may get partial credit for the outlined information.

Writing the Essay Answer:

If you have organized your details carefully, writing the answer becomes a matter of following the outline and keeping in mind the basic elements of paragraph and essay. However, if the answer is not clearly readable, you can lose points even though the content may be excellent. Write in dark ink, on one side of the paper, and leave generous margins. Leave generous amounts of space between answers as well so that you can add information later if necessary. If you are writing in an examination booklet, try to write on the right-hand side only; later you can add more information on the left side of the page. By drawing arrows, you can show where the new information fits into the answer.

Proofreading and Correcting
Essay Answers:

Recall the checklists (Chapter Six) to verify that your meaning is clear, meandering has been avoided, transitions are smooth, and writing is clear and precise. Then, if you have time, check for spelling errors, punctuation problems, and visual clarity.

KEY WORDS FREQUENTLY USED IN ESSAY EXAMINATIONS

Compare . . . .   Show similarities
Contrast . . . .   Show differences
Criticize . . . .   Show positive and negative sides
Define . . . . . .   Give the formal meaning
Describe . . . .   Tell in detail
Discuss . . . . .   Give details; both sides of issue; supporting evidence
Enumerate . .   List, number
Illustrate . . .   Explain, provide examples, support
Prove . . . . . .   Show specific evidence of truth
Summarize . .   Condense central ideas into a short paragraph
Trace . . . .   Describe chronologically; add dates as supporting evidence

INDEPENDENT ACTIVITY

Using the method described for taking an essay examination, answer the sample essay question as though it were a test. Allow yourself thirty minutes to complete the answer; check your answer by rereading portions of the section on taking essay examinations. Then look at one student's outline and response for the same question (page 103). Revise your essay answer until it pleases you.

Sample Essay Examination Question

With increasing frequency, instructors are using essay questions on mid-term and end of term examinations. Name and describe the specific steps that students may employ to improve their skills in answering essay questions. Be specific, and support your statements with reasons, wherever possible. You have a half hour to complete this test.

GROUP ACTIVITY

Share with the class or a small group your sample essay question answer.

Discuss ways in which answers might be strengthened.

Listen to the responses of other students.

From the group discussion, what generalization can you make about taking essay examinations?

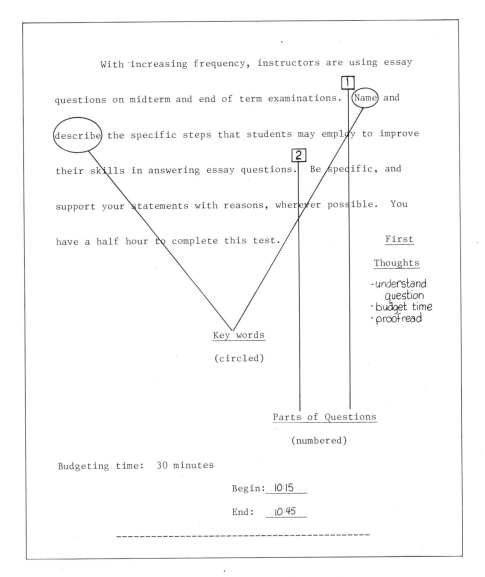

Sample Essay Examination Question (One Student's Response)

Student's Outline
 I. understand question
        circle key words
        number parts of questions
        jot down first thoughts
     Reason: prevents from misreading question

II. budget time allotted
        divide # of questions into # of minutes
        allow time for proofreading
        check clock
    Reason: prevents rushing at last minute
III. Organize ideas
        Beginning
        Middle
        Ending
    Reason: clear, logical answer
IV. Write answer
        clear, dark ink
        leave generous margins
        write on one side of page
    Reason: fill in new information later
V. Proofread
        use checklists
    Reason: prevents careless mistakes

Guiding Sentence: Students can improve their skills in answering essay questions on examinations by following five specific steps.

WRITING
THE RESEARCH PAPER

Writing the research paper is not vastly different from writing an essay or report. In an essay or report the author substantiates statements through logic, reason, example, and illustration. In a research paper the writer substantiates statements in the same way, but strengthens this support by quoting or paraphrasing other writers—authors who have written on the same or related subjects. You, in fact, already have written a research-like paper; you quoted from outside sources (appendix material) in your essay on sleep. You did not, however, use a manual of style to guide you, nor did you footnote or compile a reference list of your sources of information. To write a research paper you will need to choose a footnote or reference style and you will need to familiarize yourself with sources of information at the library.

The basic steps in writing a research paper are the same as those for writing an essay: free writing for exploring a subject; formulating a thesis statement and a tentative conclusion; subdividing the thesis into smaller, related ideas; focusing on the paragraph; *re-viewing* the draft for meaning, meandering, and mechanics; and using checklists for revision. Steps that are unique to the research paper include searching for relevant information, collecting pertinent facts and recording their specific locations, and citing the sources of the information in the research paper itself. There are numerous research techniques available, but only those that have been tested and proven effective will be presented here.

The research techniques of searching, collecting, recording, and citing information may appear as monumental tasks to you right now. However, after you have written one or two research papers and listed the sequential steps taken, you will be able to locate facts with more speed and precision. Getting to know what your library has to offer is an essential step, but this will take some time to achieve. Each time you check another source of information your familiarity with reference materials grows. And as your familiarity with reference materials grows, so does the number of reference materials. You cannot expect to keep up with even a fraction of the ever-expanding information available.

Has it ever occurred to you that our information explosion—the proliferation of reading matter that seems to be getting out of hand—is based on an alphabet of only 26 different letters? Compared to the complex symbol systems of other languages, ours can be considered a mini-alphabet. The Chinese language uses a different symbol for every word. Perhaps the mathematically oriented among you might be able to calculate the number of word combinations possible from our mere twenty-six-letter alphabet. The number of combinations is astounding. Maybe it would be easier to *picture* the progression. Visualize, if you will, letters growing into words, words developing into phrases, phrases becoming sentences, sentences becoming paragraphs, paragraphs organizing into chapters, chapters turning into books, and books bulging out of library shelves. As Doctor Frankenstein said, "I think we have created a monster."

Keeping up with the deluge of reference materials need not be a monstrous task once you know how to research and locate information. To avoid the bewilderment that comes from facing an excess of information, familiarize yourself with three or four basic information indexes and use them exclusively until you feel comfortable with them. A researcher, in one lifetime, would not exhaust a fraction of the information contained in one encyclopedia, the card catalog, the *Readers' Guide to Periodical Literature*, and the *New York Times Index*. Concentrate on using these reference sources until the nature of your subject requires you to search elsewhere.

Chances are you will be using reference sources first, when you are looking for a topic and second, after you have chosen a topic. Reading a general article in an encyclopedia will give you the overview you need either to choose or to limit a particular topic. If the subject is not one you might find in an encyclopedia, skimming a book or two on the subject will achieve the same thing. The library's card catalog lists every book alphabetically by title, author, or subject. As you look through the shelves in the area of your subject, be sure to browse left and right of your book's call number. Often that is where more relevant titles can be found. To prevent having to go back again to search through the same shelves, immediately prepare a tentative bibliography, that is, a list of books, articles, or excerpts that you may use for your project, with each item listed on a separate bibliography card.

Bibliography cards have two purposes—to help you relocate a book or article without having to go back to the card catalog or periodicals index and to provide the citation required for your research paper's bibliography, footnotes, or reference list. Each card should include the same information. Furthermore, if you list the information exactly as it will appear in your research paper's reference list you will save much time, and the task of typing the references will be less tedious.

For a book, the bibliography card must contain the author's name, the book title (underlined), the location and name of the publisher, and the year of publication. In addition, be sure to include for yourself the book's call number and the page numbers to which you will refer. In the upper right-hand corner number the cards sequentially and use that number to identify notes or photocopies from that source.

For a magazine or journal article, the bibliography card must contain the author's name, the title of the article (in quotation marks), the name of the journal or magazine (underlined), the date of publication, the volume and number of the edition (in parentheses), the page numbers to which you will refer, and your number (in the upper right-hand corner).

As you collect information, keep the bibliography cards in sequential order. If you choose to use numbered footnotes in your research paper, leave them, along with your notes and copies of articles, in sequential order as you numbered them. If, however, you will be compiling a reference list when your research is completed, at that time you can put the bibliography cards in alphabetical order. By leaving your notes and copies of articles in numerical order, you will have a cross-referenced system where information can be located easily.

When Should Research Begin?

Research is not unlike the writing process; it, too, may take varied directions and unexpected turns. Generally, the *subject* of your research dictates the sort of schedule you follow, and indeed may dictate the shape and form of the paper itself. Some topics demand instant research; they would include subjects you know little about and could do little more when free writing than pose questions. On the other hand, if you are knowledgeable in a certain subject, you might write the entire article before researching for pertinent supporting evidence. Experts in their fields and professional writers use the "write-then-research" approach. Chances are you will do some preliminary research to make a decision about a subject and to limit your topic; you will free write and formulate tentative thesis and concluding statements; you may also subdivide your thesis into smaller, related ideas; then, you will conduct additional research based on your preliminary work. Each research paper may require a different

```
Turabian, Kate L.                    1

A Manual for Writers, Fourth Ed.

Chicago:  University of Chicago Press,

1973.

Call                        Reference

Numbers                     Pages____
```

Bibliography Card for a Book

```
Collins, Carmen                      2

"The Left-Handed Notebook"

Language Arts.  Volume 58 (1), January

1981, 63-67.
```

Bibliography Card for a Magazine or Journal Article

sequence, or you may become so adept at research and writing that you devise your own method and procedures. Any procedure you choose, however, demands a technique for recording sources and information.

Taking Notes

Most published research paper guides recommend taking notes on cards—three by five, or larger. Some professional writers suggest a similar method, that is, putting one idea only on each card, keying the cards with the number you placed in the right-hand corner, then shuffling the cards around when reorganizing information. Use the card/notetaking method if it appeals to you. Markman and Waddell clearly describe its use in their book, *10 Steps in Writing the Research Paper*, published by Barron's Educational Series, Inc. Other manuals contain variations on the same technique and most bookstores carry two or more manuals. The notetaking method I am about to describe is an alternate approach—it is the one I use. *I offer it because it eliminates most of the notetaking.*

Notetaking Without Taking Notes

Notetaking without taking notes is more costly than the file card method, but it has advantages that outweigh the cost. The biggest advantage is not having to take notes in longhand; every source item is photocopied, annotated, and kept in a folder. I recommend photocopying because it eliminates some of the problems associated with writing notes on cards. Problems include taking too many notes, not taking enough, making errors in copying, and getting writer's cramp. In addition, it eliminates the dilemma of when to paraphrase from a source or when to copy the material verbatim. Students who vary their notetaking by both paraphrasing and quoting directly often cannot distinguish between the two when transcribing the information to the research paper. Finally, photocopying eliminates the problem of illegible handwriting. If you choose to try the photocopying method, you can find ways to use it wisely and to keep costs at a minimum.

Photocopying Information

The cost of photocopying is incentive enough for the researcher to learn early to discriminate between what should and what should not be copied. Often it may not be necessary to photocopy the complete article or chapter. But it is always necessary when copying a document to write the full citation, as it will appear on the bibliography card, directly on the photocopy. Write the citation in the same location on each document for consistency—the back of the last page or the top of the first are convenient locations. Staple together the pages of an article; complete a bibliography card for it; copy, in its upper right-hand corner, the number you placed on the card; then read and annotate the article.

Reading and Annotating

Skim the article for its thesis, conclusion, and related ideas. Highlight or underline portions you think you will use. Write the word "quote" in the margin next to a quotable portion. Write the word 'paraphrase" in the margin next to the section you will paraphrase. After you have collected most of your information and have annotated each source, spread the materials out and look them over. Here is where the material may dictate its own shape and form. You may find that your tentative thesis has no basis in fact because your collection of material contradicts it. If that is the case, change your thesis or your topic. If, on the other hand, your material supports your original thesis, fine. Most of the time, a tentative thesis undergoes a number of changes before the final one emerges. Put the material and your tentative thesis aside for a day before finalizing your writing plans.

Writing the Paper

When you have a thesis statement that pleases you, you will write the first draft of your research paper in much the same way as you wrote your "sleep" essay and your "A Meaningful Period" piece. This time, however, each of your guiding ideas will be expanded into a paragraph through the supportive information obtained from your research. As you develop each paragraph through quotes or paraphrases from your research, place the number of the source document from which it was taken immediately following the quote or paraphrase. In this way, you will know exactly where to find the source of information when you are ready to include the citation in your final, typed draft. Before adding reference citations to the draft, use the re-reading/writing checklists to revise and polish it.

Your instructor may require a particular approach to the documentation of your references. Chances are that he or she will ask for footnotes, that appear at the bottom of a page, plus a bibliography, or may instead suggest a "citation within the text" approach in addition to a reference list. Either way, the technicalities of each method are explained fully in any number of manuals. If you are given a choice, try the "citing within the text" method as described in *The Publication Manual of the American Psychological Association.* If you are required to use footnotes, refer to Kate Turabian's *Student's Guide for Writing College Papers.* Finally, refer to this book's checklist for preparing a professional-looking paper.

CONCLUSION

If you have come this far in *Read, Reflect, Write,* you are well on your way to independent learning. You can use this textbook again and again to practice and reinforce your newly acquired habits of flexible reading, fluent writing, and reflective thinking. When you reuse *Read, Reflect, Write* you are declaring your independence as a learner because you *are* your own teacher. The method is not different from that which the artist uses; he or she often is teacher and learner *in one.* No one would argue that an artist, sculptor, or writer is creative. Yet the most creative person admits that creativity and the development of original ideas demand attention to the more tedious, or mechanical, tasks of the craft. The painter carefully cleans the brushes; the sculptor painstakingly removes large sections of stone before attempting the finer details; writers rewrite, revise, and edit their prose or poetry. These necessary tasks need not be considered drudgery—many artists find them a relief from the even more arduous task of creating. Yes, creating is the hardest work of all. Periods of creativity must be tempered with rest, diversion, or play; no one can be creative eight hours a day, seven days a week. That is why it is important to "pace" your activities. As reader/writer, you are, after all, *an artist.*

Quick Reference:
Read, Reflect, Write
Strategies

REFERENCE LIST

Textbook Checklist

Building a Better Vocabulary
A Personal Vocabulary File
Sample Personal Vocabulary File Card

Reading Log
To Make a Two-Minute Timing Tape
Personal Reading Rate Information

Reflections Before Reading
Writing in Response to Reading
Reflections After Class

Managing Time for an Assignment
Self-Evaluation
Preparing a Professional-Looking Paper

How to Assay an Essay
How to Develop an Essay
How to Use the Assay Method to Capture
the Meaning of a Textbook Chapter

Progress Review
Paragraph Checklist
Checklist for Meaning
Checklist for Avoiding Meandering
Mechanics Checklist
Revision Checklist
Essay Examination Checklist

TEXTBOOK CHECKLIST

Title _____

Author _____

Publisher _____

Publication date _____

Number of chapters _____

Number of pages _____

I. Check the items found in the textbook.

Foreword _____   Appendix _____

Introduction _____   Index _____

References _____   Other _____

Glossary _____

II. Read the Table of Contents.
Notice the major divisions of the book.
Leaf through the book. What is the format? Do the chapters follow a pattern?
What kind of pattern? Look at each chapter. *Write* one sentence describing
the format or pattern of the chapters.

_____

_____

III. Check the subdivisions found in the chapters.

Introduction _____   Summaries _____

Subheadings _____   Questions   _____

Activities   _____   Exercises   _____

IV. Read the Foreword and the Introduction to the book.

BUILDING A BETTER VOCABULARY

The moment you encounter a new word, take some action.

First, if you own the book, *underline* the new word. If it's not your book, *write* the new word down.

Second, *try to get the meaning from the context.* Read the sentence in which the word appears. Does the sentence reveal the meaning of the word?

Third, look through your textbook (or check your textbook checklist) for a *glossary.* Glossaries define terms as they are used in the context of your book.

Fourth, use a *dictionary* if no glossary exists. Try to find the definition that fits the context.

Fifth, make a permanent record of the word and its definition in your *Personal Vocabulary File.*

A PERSONAL VOCABULARY FILE

A personal vocabulary file serves three purposes. As a memory technique, it enables you to make associations with words you already know. As a resource, it expands your knowledge by adding to your supply of working words. As a study skill, it stores definitions for reviewing for examinations or when writing reports and papers.

Use a small looseleaf notebook or three-by-five cards or pads. Using the same size paper or cards for all your entries will make the system more efficient and easy to handle, and the information will be readily available for quick reference.

1. On one side of a card, print or type the new word. If the word is difficult to pronounce, add the phonetic spelling from the dictionary.

Front of Card:

```
WORD:   denotation


    PHONETIC SPELLING (as given in dictionary):


            (dē' nō tā' shən)
```

Back of Card:

```
    DEFINITION:   The explicit meaning of a word, as
opposed to its connotation.
    PERSONAL MEMORY LINK:  Strong Association

                           Related Idea

                           Diagram or Drawing

                           Synonym and/or Antonym

    SENTENCE:
```

2. On the other side of the card, write the definition that best fits the meaning of the sentence in which the word appears.

3. Add a personal memory link. Choose one or more of the following ways to link the meaning of the new word to something you already know: jot down the first strong association that occurs to you; write down a related idea; draw a diagram or picture; reflect on the new word and try to call up a *synonym*, a word that is similar in meaning, or an *antonym*, a word that is opposite in meaning.

4. Finally, write an original sentence using the new word, or copy the sentence in which it appeared (if you believe the sentence will be useful when you are studying for an examination in the subject).

READING LOG

In your Reading Log, include the following information for each reading session:

Date: _____

Starting time: _____

Stopping time: _____

Number of pages read (e.g., pp. 1-10): _____

Write one sentence in response to the reading: _____

_____

_____

1. You may summarize what you have read.
2. You may react to the text.
3. You may comment on your feelings after reading.
4. You may copy a particular sentence (for any reason) from the text.
5. You may choose another way of responding.

TO MAKE A TWO-MINUTE TIMING TAPE

1. Turn on the tape and watch the clock.
2. When the second hand is on twelve, say, "Start" into the microphone. Keep watching the clock.
3. When the second hand reaches twelve again, after *two* minutes, say, "Stop."
4. Turn off the machine and rewind the tape.

Use the two-minute tape to monitor your reading flexibility. When two minutes pass, count the number of words you have read, *then divide the number by two.* This is your actual reading rate for the passage. To check your understanding, complete the Writing in Response to Reading.

PERSONAL READING RATE INFORMATION

Date: _____

Starting time: _____

Stopping time: _____

Total number of minutes: _____

Number of words per minute: _____

REFLECTIONS BEFORE READING

Reflect for a few minutes each time you begin reading, and jot down answers to the following questions:

Why am I reading this particular piece?
What do I want to know?
What do I already know about the subject?
What is the best way to read this material?

WRITING IN RESPONSE TO READING

Upon completing the reading of a passage, do the following exercise:

1. Quickly write your impression of the author's main points or central ideas. Continue writing freely for two minutes, or as long as ideas continue to occur.
2. Write a summary of your response to item one (above) in a single sentence.
3. Write one sentence or more from the passage that tells what the selection is about: *This is what I'm going to say.*
4. Write one sentence or more from the passage that reveals the conclusion: *This is what I have said.*
5. List the ways in which the ideas expressed in the passage relate (or do not relate) to you, your life, your ideas.

REFLECTIONS AFTER CLASS

Before reviewing class notes or completing the assignment, write for two minutes to answer the questions below.

What was the most important thing I learned today? Why is it important? How might this knowledge affect me? Was anything unclear about today's session? List all questions that occur to you.

While reviewing class notes, look for beginnings, middles, and endings. Mark in different colors the *this is what I am going to say* and *this is what I've said* statements.

After reviewing class notes and completing the assignment, write answers to the questions below.

Have all my questions (above) been answered? If not, place a check next to the questions to be asked in class at the next session. How successful was today's work? How can I improve it?

MANAGING TIME
FOR AN ASSIGNMENT

Within a day of receiving the assignment, preread your assignment carefully. Free write for a few minutes, jotting down notes, ideas, and first thoughts about how you will deal with the assignment. First thoughts may include a sequence of steps you may have to take even before beginning the actual work, particularly if outside research is needed. When you run out of ideas, put the assignment aside.

The following day, reread your original notes and free write again, adding thoughts and ideas as they occur. When ideas run dry, put the assignment aside. If outside research is required, jot down the sources you will need to locate, and carry the list of sources with you.

On each succeeding day, before you actually begin to write a first draft, reread and add new ideas and material to your notes. When you are in the library or bookstore, skim the shelves for information related to your topic. Keep pen and pad handy at all times, even in front of the television set, to jot down ideas that may occur spontaneously.

SELF-EVALUATION

In self-evaluation, you will be commenting on your own writing and establishing your own goals for improvement.

1. How much time did you spend on this paper?
2. What did you try to improve on this paper? How successful were you? If you have questions about what you were trying to do, what are they?
3. What are the strengths of your paper? Place a check mark beside those passages you feel are very good.
4. What are the weaknesses, if any, of your paper? Place an *X* beside passages you would like corrected or revised. Place an *X* over any punctuation, spelling, usage, etc., where you need help or clarification.
5. What *one thing* will you do to improve your next piece of writing?
6. What would you do *differently* on this paper if you had more time?
7. Write a one-sentence summary of this self-evaluation.

PREPARING A PROFESSIONAL-LOOKING PAPER

If your instructor does not specify a particular format for written reports and papers, this one can be used for most subjects and courses.

1. Use plain white, unruled paper.
2. Type everything double-spaced. (Also, check a style manual for extended quotations and footnote formats.)
3. Type your name, class, and date on three separate lines in the upper left-hand corner of the first page.
4. Begin typing halfway down the first page with your title in capital letters.
5. Type your last name or a word from the title in the uppermost left-hand corner of every page except the first.
6. Type the page number in the upper right-hand corner of every page except the first.
7. Leave generous 1 1/2 inch margins on all sides.
8. Make corrections carefully by drawing one line through a word and inserting the correction above it. If you omit a letter or word, use a *caret* (an upside down *v*) to point it out, and print the omission neatly above it.
9. If there is a distracting number of corrections on a page, retype the entire page.

10. If you choose to use a cover page, place your name, class, and date at the upper left-hand corner, and the title in capital letters in the center of the page. Begin page one, halfway down, but eliminate the title if you use a cover page.

HOW TO ASSAY AN ESSAY

Preparation:

Read the title and author's name.

Reflect briefly on both title and author.

Write freely, describing your expectations of the essay.

1. What does the title reveal?
2. Try to predict or anticipate some of the information that might be included in the essay.
3. What does the author's name or background (if known) suggest?
4. Try to predict the author's point of view or "slant" on the subject.

Step One: Recognizing The Thesis

Read the essay until you come to the author's thesis: the *this is what I am going to say* statement.

Reflect: A thesis tells what the essay will be about. You may have to read one or more paragraphs to find it, but often it follows the introduction. Sometimes it is implied rather than stated. In that case, the reader may have to put it into words.

1. Does the thesis you found tell what the essay will be about?
2. Does the thesis reveal something of the author's viewpoint, feeling, or attitude toward the subject?

Write down the thesis statement. Use the author's words if the thesis is stated; use your own words if it is implied.

If, in the first two paragraphs, there are no clues to the author's thesis, continue with the *assay* then, when you have completed step three, reread and complete step one.

Step Two: Recognizing
The Conclusion

Read the last paragraph of the essay for the author's concluding statement: *this is what I have said.*

Reflect: If the last paragraph does not reveal the summary or conclusion, read a paragraph or two before it until you find the concluding statement.

    1. Does the statement summarize, conclude, or tell something about what was said?

    2. Does the statement include the author's viewpoint or attitude toward the subject?

Write down the concluding statement. Use the author's words if the conclusion is explicit; use your own words if it is implied or suggested.

    If, in the last two paragraphs, there are no clues to the author's conclusion, continue with the *assay* then, when you have completed step three, reread and complete this section.

Reread the thesis and the concluding statement.

Reflect: Is there a relationship between the two statements? Are they compatible or in agreement? Or, do they seem unrelated? Do they contain opposing or incompatible ideas?

    If the statements seem to be unrelated or not complementary, reread the opening and closing paragraphs to reconsider your choices of thesis and conclusion. At this point, you may wish to choose another sentence for either the thesis or the conclusion. You may decide to change one or the other, or you may conclude that your original choices were best.

Write: If you have chosen another statement for either the thesis or conclusion, write down your final choices.

Step Three: Recognizing Smaller,
Related Ideas

Read the first sentence of each paragraph.

Reflect briefly on the sentence and its relationship to the thesis.

Write each of the sentences in the order of appearance, leaving four or five spaces on your paper between each sentence.

    If you have not already done so, look up all words you do not understand or cannot get meaning for from the context of the sentences in which they appear.

Write one sentence in your own words to summarize or tell what the essay is about. *Remember, the summary will be written from the information included in the thesis, conclusion, and first sentences of each paragraph.*

If you have not, as yet, determined the author's thesis and/or conclusion, study the extracted sentences then reread and complete steps one and two.

HOW TO DEVELOP AN ESSAY

1. Formulate a thesis statement,
2. write a tentative conclusion,
3. subdivide the thesis into smaller, related ideas,
4. develop a paragraph for each of the related ideas.

A Thesis Worksheet:
For a Personal Essay

Read your notes and jottings for your proposed essay.
Reflect on the topic by answering the following questions:

1. *What* happened? *Who* was present?
2. *Where* and *When* did the event or period take place?
3. *Why* did it happen?
4. *How* do I feel about the experience?

Write freely in answer to each question.

Subdividing a Thesis into Smaller, Related Ideas

One way of subdividing a statement into separate, meaningful segments is by asking direct questions, such as

Who or *What* is (are) the subject(s)?
[Subjects are the persons, places, things, or ideas an author mentions.]
What is (are) the subject(s) doing?
When or *Where* does the action take place?
Why or *How* does the action occur?
Write your thoughts randomly and quickly, as they occur.

HOW TO USE THE ASSAY
METHOD TO CAPTURE
THE MEANING
OF A TEXTBOOK CHAPTER

Preparation

Read the chapter's title, subtitles, and headings. Glance at charts and diagrams; read their titles or headings.

Reflect on what you have read.

Write one sentence in which you anticipate or *predict* what the chapter will be about.

Step One: Recognizing
The Chapter's Purpose

Read the beginning paragraph(s) for a statement of purpose or thesis (this is what the chapter will be about).

Reflect: Is there a statement that tells what the chapter is about?

Write down the statement, or use your own words.

   If a statement of purpose is not evident, go to step two.

Step Two: Recognizing
The Conclusion

Read the last paragraph or two for a concluding statement. Read the end-of-chapter questions or exercises.

Reflect on the questions; this is the information you are to recall.

Write the conclusion or summary statement as written, or in your own words.

   If a conclusion is not evident, go to step three.

Step Three: Recognizing
Smaller, Related Ideas

Read headings and first sentences of each paragraph.

Reflect briefly on the relationship of heading to first sentences.

Write headings and first sentences in order of appearance. Indent leading sentences and leave four or five spaces between each.

   If you have not done so, look up all words you do not understand or for which you cannot get the meaning from the context. Check the textbook glossary before looking in the dictionary.

Write two or three sentences to summarize or tell what the chapter is about.

If purpose statement and/or conclusion have not been determined, study the extracted sentences then reread and complete steps one and two.

PROGRESS REVIEW

Take a few moments, periodically, to free write in answer to the following *Progress Review Questions*:

How have your daily reading and writing practices changed since you began this book?

Have you been keeping up with daily journal writing and pleasure reading?

Are you monitoring your reading habits and writing processes?

Where have you made the most progress?

In which areas do you need more practice?

How close are you to becoming an independent learner?

Look through the table of contents of this text; which chapters need rereading?

How are you doing in your other courses?

What can you take from this book to improve your understanding and responses to other academic subjects?

How can you move beyond this text to even more creative ways of learning?

PARAGRAPH CHECKLIST

READER'S QUESTIONS	WRITER'S QUESTIONS
Purpose	
Is the purpose of each of the author's paragraphs evident?	What is the purpose of each of my paragraphs?
Does each paragraph achieve its purpose?	Does each of my paragraphs achieve its purpose?
How can the purpose of each paragraph be improved?	

Order

Are the sentences in each paragraph arranged logically?

What is the best arrangement of sentences in each paragraph?

Is there enough information, or do I have unanswered questions?

Does each of my paragraphs contain enough information for the reader?

How can the order of sentences in a paragraph be improved?

Transitions

Does each sentence flow smoothly and naturally to the next one?

Does each sentence flow smoothly and naturally to the next one?

Does each paragraph flow smoothly and naturally to the next one?

Does each paragraph flow smoothly and naturally to the next one?

How can the flow, through the use of transitions, be improved?

CHECKLIST FOR MEANING

Does the chapter or essay have a beginning, middle, and ending?
Is there a thesis statement or a *This is what I am going to say* statement?
Is there a concluding, summarizing, or *This is what I have said* statement?

CHECKLIST FOR AVOIDING MEANDERING

Does each paragraph have a guiding idea?
Is the guiding idea related to the thesis?
Is the guiding idea expressed in the guiding sentence?
Do all the paragraph's sentences expand upon the guiding idea?
Are each of the paragraph's guiding ideas related to the thesis?
Are each of the paragraph's guiding ideas related to one another?
Is there a relationship among thesis, conclusion, and guiding ideas?

MECHANICS CHECKLIST

(To be used in conjunction with a writing handbook)

Does each sentence have a subject and verb?
Is there agreement between subject and verb in each sentence?
Are pronouns used correctly?
Is there agreement between pronoun and verb in each sentence?
Are adverbs and adjectives used correctly?
Has misuse of punctuation been corrected?
Have misspellings been corrected?

REVISION CHECKLIST

Delete useless information.
Cross out words that merely occupy space.
Use one word instead of two or three wherever possible.
Replace difficult words with more common words.
Divide long sentences into shorter statements (as long as each statement has both a subject and a verb).
Change negative statements to positive ones, if possible.
Make general statements more specific.
Substitute another word for "very."
Use the words "a lot" and "all right" instead of the incorrect single-word spellings.

ESSAY EXAMINATION CHECKLIST

1. Be certain you understand the meaning of the question.
2. Budget the time allotted for the test.
3. Organize ideas before writing the answer.
4. Write the answer clearly.
5. Proofread and correct the answer.

Appendix

Photo by Carmen Collins

READING PASSAGE NUMBER ONE
HAPPINESS AND YOUR OWN I.Q.*

Taking charge of yourself involves putting to rest some very prevalent myths. At the top of the list is the notion that intelligence is measured by your ability to solve complex problems; to read, write, and compute at certain levels; and to resolve abstract equations quickly. This vision of intelligence predicates formal education and bookish excellence as the true measures of self-fulfillment. It encourages a kind of intellectual snobbery that has brought with it some demoralizing results. We have come to believe that someone who has more educational merit badges, who is a whiz at some form of scholastic discipline (math, science, a huge vocabulary, a memory for superfluous facts, a fast reader) is "intelligent." Yet mental hospitals are clogged with patients who have all of the properly lettered credentials—as well as many who don't. A truer barometer of intelligence is an effective, happy life lived each day and each present moment of every day.

If you are happy, if you live each moment for everything it's worth, then you are an intelligent person. Problem solving is a useful adjunct to your happiness, but if you know that given your inability to resolve a particular concern you can still choose happiness for yourself, or at a minimum refuse to choose unhappiness, then you are intelligent. You are intelligent because you have the ultimate weapon against the big N.B.D. Yep—*Nervous Break Down.*

Perhaps you will be surprised to learn that there is no such thing as a nervous breakdown. Nerves don't break down. Cut someone open and look for the broken nerves. They never show up. "Intelligent" people do not have N.B.D.'s because they are in charge of themselves. They know how to choose happiness over depression, because they know how to deal with the *problems* of their lives. Notice I didn't say *solve* the problems. Rather than measuring their intelligence on their ability to *solve* the problem, they measure it on their capacity for maintaining themselves as happy and worthy, whether the problem gets solved or not.

You can begin to think of yourself as truly intelligent on the basis of how you choose to feel in the face of trying circumstances. The life struggles are pretty much the same for each of us. Everyone who is involved with other human beings in any social context has similar difficulties. Disagreements, conflicts, and compromises are a part of what it means to be human. Similarly, money, growing old, sickness, deaths, natural disasters, and accidents are all events which present problems to virtually all human beings. But some people are able to make it, to avoid

*Abridged from pp. 8-13 in *Your Erroneous Zones* by Wayne W. Dyer (Funk & Wagnalls, Publishers). Copyright © 1976 by Wayne W. Dyer. Reprinted by permission of Harper & Row Publishers, Inc.

immobilizing dejection and unhappiness despite such occurrences, while others collapse, become inert or have an N.B.D. Those who recognize problems as a human condition and don't measure happiness by an absence of problems are the most intelligent kind of humans we know; also, the most rare.

Learning to take total charge of yourself will involve a whole new thinking process, one which may prove difficult because too many forces in our society conspire against individual responsibility. You must trust in your own ability to feel emotionally whatever you choose to feel at any time in your life. This is a radical notion. You've probably grown up believing that you can't control your own emotions; that anger, fear and hate, as well as love, ecstasy and joy are things that happen to you. An individual doesn't control these things, he accepts them. When sorrowful events occur, you just naturally feel sorrow, and hope that some happy events will come along so that you can feel good very soon. . . .

Feelings are not just emotions that happen to you. Feelings are reactions you choose to have. If you are in charge of your own emotions, you don't have to choose self-defeating reactions. Once you learn that you can feel what you choose to feel, you will be on the road to "intelligence"—a road where there are no bypaths that lead to N.B.D.'s. This road will be new because you'll see a given emotion as a choice rather than as a condition of life. This is the very heart and soul of personal freedom. . . .

You have the power to think whatever you choose to allow into your head. If something just "pops" into your head (You choose to put it there, though you may not know why), you still have the power to make it go away, and therefore you still control your mental world . . . . You alone control what enters your head as a thought. If you don't believe this, just answer this question, "If you don't control your thoughts, who does?" Is it your spouse, or your boss, or your mamma? And if *they* control what you think, then send them off for therapy and *you* will instantly get better. But you really know otherwise. You and only you control your thinking apparatus (other than under extreme kinds of brainwashing or conditioning experimentation settings which are not a part of your life). Your thoughts are your own, uniquely yours to keep, change, share, or contemplate. No one else can get inside your head and have your own thoughts as you experience them. You do indeed control your thoughts, and your brain is your own to use as you so determine. . . .

You cannot have a feeling (emotion) without first having experienced a thought. Take away your brain and your ability to "feel" is wiped out. A feeling is a physical reaction to a thought. If you cry, or blush, or increase your heartbeat, or any of an interminable list of potential emotional reactions, you have first had a signal from your thinking center. Once your thinking center is damaged or short-circuited, you cannot experience emotional reactions. . . .

If you control your thoughts, and your feelings come from your thoughts, then you are capable of controlling your own feelings. And you control your feelings by working on the thoughts that preceded them. Simply put, you believe that things or people make you unhappy, but this is not accurate. You make yourself unhappy because of the thoughts that you have about the people or things in your life. Becoming a free and healthy person involves learning to *think* differently. Once you can change your thoughts, your new feelings will begin to emerge, and you will have taken the first step on the road to your personal freedom.

READING PASSAGE
NUMBER ONE
WORDS-PER-MINUTE
RATE CHART

MINUTES AND SECONDS	WORDS PER MINUTE (WPM) (APPROXIMATE)
10 minutes	104
9 minutes, 30 seconds	109
9 minutes	116
8 minutes, 30 seconds	122
8 minutes	130
7 minutes, 30 seconds	139
7 minutes	149
6 minutes, 30 seconds	160
6 minutes	175
5 minutes, 30 seconds	189
5 minutes	208
4 minutes, 30 seconds	231
4 minutes	260
3 minutes, 30 seconds	297
3 minutes	347
2 minutes, 30 seconds	416
2 minutes	520
1 minute, 30 seconds	693
1 minute	1040

READING PASSAGE NUMBER TWO
NOBODY'S PERFECT:
THE TRAP OF SELF-CRITICISM*

Long before the psychology of self-esteem taught us how important it is to have a decent opinion of ourselves, Mark Twain summed up the theory's

*Dr. Hendrie Weisinger, Norman M. Lobsenz, *Nobody's Perfect* (Los Angeles: Stratford Press, Inc., 1981), pp. 213-19.

basic principles in a single insightful remark: "A man," he wrote, "cannot be comfortable without his own approval." But it often seems harder to gain that ultimate accolade than to win the approval of others. The harshest criticism many of us receive is the criticism we give ourselves.

In her essay on self-forgiveness author Ardis Whitman says, "We brood over what we've done and what we've left undone; over the hurts we've brought to others and the damage we've brought to ourselves; over . . . the inability to get rid of whatever faults we may have." Most of us are willing to forgive the failings of others. Why can't we forgive our own? To answer that question—to become aware of the dynamics of self-criticism—we must first understand how the relationship between criticism and self-image works.

Paradoxically, one's concept of one's "self" does not develop from the inside out, but rather is fashioned from the outside in. "O, wad some Pow'r the giftie gie us/To see oursels as others see us!" Robert Burns exclaimed. But that is precisely the way we do "see oursels." It is how we think that we appear to others, and how others judge us, that is largely responsible for the self-image we construct. And because we internalize the standards and opinions imposed on us by others, we tend to take on their attitudes and measure our own behavior by them.

. . .Repeated criticism in the formative years of life from those who are emotionally important to us can lead to the development of a poor self-concept. A child who grows up with destructively criticizing parents, for example, is likely to internalize the judgments those parents voice and the way in which he thinks they perceive him. But it is not only the *content* of parental criticisms that is made a part of the self-image. The child is also likely to internalize the criticism *process* he or she has been exposed to, and thus become a destructively self-criticizing adult.

In short, self-critics are simultaneously both givers and takers of criticism, quick to berate themselves in destructive ways and also to interpret that criticism destructively. That is why self-criticism can be doubly damaging unless we understand how to deal with it effectively—how to reject it when it does us a disservice, and how to make use of it when it is to our advantage. . . .

Man has an inherent need to master his environment, to deal with the challenges of living in a competent way. One of the useful purposes self-criticism serves is to help us evaluate our actions so that we can constructively answer that constantly recurring inner question, *How am I doing?* But the person who has internalized a destructive approach to self-criticism sabotages its useful function. He or she has *learned* to do so as a child through years of exposure to negative criticism.

A child, for example, may be rewarded with love and approval for outstanding performance—a fine report card, athletic success, good behavior. But when parents react to that youngster's occasional shortcoming or deficiency with anxiety, disappointment or rebuke, the child will most likely interpret that response as a punishment or rejection. Not surprisingly, such a child becomes especially sensitive to failure, whether real or imagined. He or she actually begins to anticipate failure, to closely monitor his or her behavior to see if it threatens to occur. The child seeks to acknowledge failure before his or her parents do.

This pattern becomes a learned habit. It represents the first characteristic of destructive self-criticism: looking for defects, anticipating mistakes—in short, focusing on the negatives in one's life. By thus perpetuating a poor self-image, the self-critic blocks possibilities for change and growth. A man, for instance, clings to a relatively secure but dead-end job because he is afraid that if he accepts a more challenging one he may fail. A woman stays in a boring marriage because she fears she isn't clever or pretty enough to attract another man.

Focusing on negatives has two major consequences for thought and action. One is the tendency to jump to the conclusion that a single mistake or failure will be endlessly repeated. When something goes wrong, the destructive self-critic says, *That always happens to me . . . I can never do anything right.* This emotional constriction tends to make the self-critic avoid any experience or turn away from any opportunity which does not have a successful outcome firmly guaranteed. Since failure is equated with fear of rejection, he or she forestalls rejection by essaying nothing which might fail. The predictable result is stagnation. . . .

Many men and women think they have failed when they do not live up to their own unrealistic expectations. Though they can almost never meet the rigorous standards they set for themselves, says psychiatrist David Burns, they nevertheless have an "irrational belief that they must be perfect to be accepted." (Or *self*-accepted. A well-known woman writer recently confessed that "sometimes, when I really want to drive myself bananas, the judge inside myself adds that I'm not *self-critical* enough.")

This need to be perfect also stems from childhood experiences of parental criticism. To bolster their own self-esteem, parents often expect a child to achieve results beyond the youngster's desires or abilities. A mother may push her average-student daughter to make the Dean's List; a father may press his athletically uncoordinated son to go out for the varsity football team. Any behavior that falls short of these expectations, no matter how great an achievement in itself, is apt to be considered a "failure" and provoke destructive criticism. Eventually the frustrated youngster decides (again unconsciously) that in order not to be criticized—i.e., rejected—he or she must always strive for and achieve nothing less than perfection.

When internalized in adulthood, this need to be perfect means one has replaced one's parents' unrealistically high expectations with one's own. No matter how well such a person performs, he or she is apt to evaluate that performance in terms of an all-or-nothing self-critical put-down. David Burns singles out such thinking as "perhaps the most common mental distortion" of perfectionists: "They evaluate their experiences in a dichotomous manner, seeing things as either all-black or all-white; intermediate shades of grey do not seem to exist."

In other words, the need to be perfect places a person in a self-destructive double bind. If one fails to meet the unrealistic expectation, one has failed; but if one *does* meet it, one feels no glow of achievement for one has only done what was expected. There is no objective way to measure effort or improvement, no chance to relish success, no reason to build up one's self-image.

"Should" statements are often a hallmark of this attitude: "It wasn't too bad a job but it *should* have been better." "I didn't get as much done as I *should* have." Such statements are damaging enough when applied to actions, but they can be much more damaging when applied to feelings. Self-critics often disparage themselves for feeling a certain way—angry, hostile, even happy—because they "shouldn't" feel that way. But when we destructively criticize ourselves for feelings, we create a no-win situation. Denying the legitimacy of our feelings inhibits the health or necessary expression of emotion; reproaching ourselves for our feelings without reason makes us out to be some kind of villain.

READING PASSAGE
NUMBER TWO
WORDS-PER-MINUTE
RATE CHART

MINUTES AND SECONDS	WORDS PER MINUTE (WPM) (APPROXIMATE)
10 minutes	125
9 minutes, 30 seconds	132
9 minutes	139
8 minutes, 30 seconds	147
8 minutes	156
7 minutes, 30 seconds	167
7 minutes	179
6 minutes, 30 seconds	192
6 minutes	208
5 minutes, 30 seconds	227
5 minutes	250
4 minutes, 30 seconds	278
4 minutes	312

MINUTES AND SECONDS	WORDS PER MINUTE (WPM) (APPROXIMATE)
3 minutes, 30 seconds	357
3 minutes	416
2 minutes, 30 seconds	500
2 minutes	625
1 minute, 30 seconds	833
1 minute	1250

THE RHYTHMS AND LEVELS OF SLEEP*

All humans periodically lose consciousness in sleep. We are so accustomed to the normal rhythm of sleep and wakefulness that we do not consider how strange it is that the consciousness on which we pride ourselves, and which we regard as the very essence of individual personality, should be suspended altogether for about a third of our lives. Of all human behaviors, sleep is one of the most mystifying and least understood. Until the past few decades, most people supposed that sleep was the time when the brain rested. Scientists now know that the sleeping brain is as active as the waking one, and that at certain times during the sleep period it is furiously at work in the processing of information. The belief that sleep is the consequence of fatigue has been found to be, at best, an oversimplification. Nor is it the function of sleep to give relief from an overload of sensory stimulation during the waking day. Volunteers who submitted to experiments isolating them from all sensory stimulation have been placed in separate rooms that were completely darkened and soundproofed; they were even supplied with gloves to eliminate tactile sensations. The first day, with sensory stimulation completely absent, they slept for an average of between twelve and fourteen hours. The explanation for this probably lies in the fact that the volunteers had nothing to do except to sleep; certainly it could not have been the result of any need for relief from sensory stimulation.

Scientists do not even know how much sleep people need. A generation ago, most hygiene books stated that adults require eight hours of sleep each night. Sleep researchers are now discovering, though, that the amount of sleep needed is very much an individual matter. Cases are

*From *Humankind* by Peter Farb. Copyright © 1978 by Peter Farb. Reprinted by permission of Houghton Mifflin Company and Jonathan Cape Limited.

known of extremely active people who for half a century never slept more than four hours a night. On the other hand, even a healthy person may need as much as seventeen hours on occasion. Claims have been made from time to time concerning people who supposedly went for extremely long periods with no sleep at all, but most such cases never survived scientific scrutiny. The longest verified case on record is that of a high-school youth who was kept under constant observation by researchers from the Stanford University Sleep Laboratory, and who stayed awake for 264 consecutive hours—exactly eleven days—without exhibiting any serious emotional changes. In fact, he remained so alert that on the last night of his vigil he beat one of the researchers in every game they played in a penny arcade. Nor did he exhibit any exceptional need to make up sleep afterward. Following a first sleep lasting only about fourteen hours, he stayed up for 24 hours before going to sleep again, this time for a mere eight hours.

Sleep researchers have so far failed to answer fully the obvious question: What lures us every night from our work, our leisure activities, our family and friends into the solitary world of sleep? It is difficult to believe that human beings spend about a third of their lives in a state that has no function. Yet one researcher became so pessimistic about the failure to pinpoint the functions of sleep that he came to wonder whether it had any function at all:

> If sleep does not serve an absolutely vital function, then it is the biggest mistake the evolutionary process ever made. Sleep precludes hunting for and consuming food. It is incompatible with procreation. It produces vulnerability to attack from enemies. Sleep interferes with every voluntary motor act in the repertoire of coping mechanisms. How could natural selection with its irrevocable logic have "permitted" the animal kingdom to pay the price of sleep for no good reason? In fact, the behavior of sleep is so apparently maladaptive that one can only wonder why some other condition did not evolve to satisfy whatever need it is that sleep satisfies.

Almost no scientists, however, believe that natural selection plays such tantalizing games with human behavior. Before going into some possible functions that can be postulated for sleep, I want to explain in more detail what sleep is.

The modern understanding of sleep began quite by accident in 1952, when a graduate student was assigned to observe the eyelids of sleeping volunteers to see whether any movement occurred. He observed that at certain times during the night the eyeballs of sleepers darted about furiously beneath the closed lids. (Eye movements are very easy to detect, even when the lids are closed; ask someone to perform these movements and see for yourself.) Such activity was totally unexpected, since sleep had long been thought to be a time of quiescence, not one in which the brain was actively generating eye movements that were often faster than could be produced by a waking person. Since then, much more has been learned about rapid eye movement (technically known as "REM") during certain stages of sleep. REM sleep is always accompanied by very distinctive brain-wave patterns, a marked increase in blood flow and in the temperature of the brain, irregular breathing, convulsive twitches of the face and fingertips, and the erection of the penis and clitoris. REM sleep is active sleep, even though the large muscles of the body are completely relaxed. The other kind of sleep is known as "NREM" (that is, non-REM). During this state, breathing is regular, body movement is generally absent, and brain activity is low. Perception shuts down because the senses are no longer gathering information and communicating it to the brain. NREM sleep is sometimes called "quiet sleep" but in one respect that is not so; snoring occurs during this stage.

A number of curious experiences occur at the onset of sleep. A person just about to go to sleep may experience an electric shock, a flash of light, or a crash of thunder—but the most common sensation is that of floating or falling, which is why "falling asleep" is a scientifically valid description. A nearly universal occurrence at the beginning of sleep (although not everyone recalls it) is a sudden, uncoordinated jerk of the head, the limbs, or even the entire body. Most people tend to think of going to sleep as a slow slippage into oblivion, but the onset of sleep is not gradual at all. It happens in an instant. One moment the individual is awake, the next moment not.

The first period of sleep is always NREM. It consists of four stages, during each of which the sleeper becomes more remote from the sensory environment. Children in particular are virtually unwakenable at the fourth stage. Even if they can finally be roused, it may be several minutes before they return to awareness. This deepest fourth stage is the period during which most of the talking in one's sleep, sleep-walking, night terrors, and bed-wetting by children take place. After the fourth stage, the sleeper retraces all the stages back to lighter sleep. The downward progression into the first deep sleep is smooth, but the upward progression is marked by irregular jumps from one stage to the other. The first REM period begins about seventy or eighty minutes after a person has fallen asleep and usually lasts for only about ten minutes. The entire NREM-REM cycle averages about ninety minutes, but with some individuals it is as short as seventy minutes and with others as long as 110. The two kinds of sleep—as different from each other as sleep is from wakefulness—continue to alternate throughout the night. With each cycle, the amount of REM sleep gradually increases, to the degree that it may become as long as sixty minutes just before awakening, whereas the amount of NREM sleep decreases markedly. An adult who sleeps seven and a half hours spends from one and a half to two hours of that period in REM sleep, mostly toward the end of the sleep period.

The new view of sleep that has emerged in the past few decades from numerous laboratories is not one of sleep as "death's counterfeit," as Shakespeare put it. Sleep is not passive in the sense that it is the absence of something characteristic of wakefulness. Rather, it is an active state in which the brain is never at rest. One theory about human sleep assigns different functions to the two kinds of sleep. NREM sleep apparently does the things that have traditionally been assigned by common sense to all sleep: growth, repair to the body's tissues, and the synthesis of proteins. NREM sleep is a biological necessity; without it, an individual eventually would collapse. When someone is deprived of sleep, NREM sleep is usually made up first. And until the deprivation is compensated for, that person feels lethargic and less able than usual to carry out physical tasks.

REM sleep, in contrast, apparently restores the neural processes underlying consciousness; it is mental rather than physical. People deprived of it are not physically lethargic but emotionally irritable; they usually perform poorly in concentration and learning tests. REM sleep appears to be essential to integrate recently learned material into longterm memory. Students who stay up all night cramming for an examination the next day usually do not do as well as those who have had some sleep. The explanation is that the students have momentarily learned a lot of new facts, but these facts cannot be remembered unless they have been processed during sleep for incorporation into the memory. REM sleep also seems to help people cope with day-to-day stress. Experiments have shown that volunteers who were exposed to stressful situations had a sharply increased need for REM sleep, during which time they apparently made peace with the traumatic experiences. Such experiments offer fresh evidence that sleep is one of the most active parts of a person's day.

STATES OF AWARENESS*

Usually, we think of awareness as the sensory perception of the sights, sounds, and smells around us. But our awareness extends to many more perceptions. If we take the time to look into ourselves, we will become aware, first, of a number of bodily sensations. We will notice the rhythm of our breathing and heartbeat, feel stomach movements, the saliva in our mouth, the texture and weight of our clothing, small aches, itches, perhaps even passing pains. Besides these physical sensations, we also become aware of vague emotions—drifts toward pleasure, irritation, or boredom. And, depending on our emotional makeup, we may be acutely or dimly aware of the passage of time, the future, our own mortality, the continuity of our awareness, and the essential separateness of our conscious self.

*Gardner Lindzey, Calvin S. Hall, and Richard F. Thompson, *Psychology,* 2nd ed. (New York: Worth Publishers, Inc., 1978), pp. 171-72, 337-38.

Though it is difficult for individuals to describe their self-awareness with any degree of precision, the sense of one's own being is nonetheless animated by a great warmth, immediacy, and richness. This complex, often poignant, perception of oneself is particularly evident in times of emotional fullness, as when making love or when feeling great sorrow. However, it is always present to some extent, even in the dullest, most ordinary moments of one's life. Psychology is just beginning to develop tools to observe and register these aspects of awareness. We still must rely in large part on verbal descriptions, supplemented by relatively simple recordings of heart rate, respiration, gland secretions, and the brain's overall electrical activity.

The familiar level of awareness is conscious thought. Even if we sit quietly and become introspective, we are always thinking. Ideas, no matter how trivial, continually pass through our awareness. Most normal thinking, furthermore, appears to be accompanied by behavioral responses—when we think our tongue and throat muscles usually make small movements. If we are not actively thinking, we are probably daydreaming. The average person has about 200 daydreams every day.

Awareness, then, is the sum of everything one can discover about one's experience at a given time. There is, of course, much more to a person than immediate awareness. We also have innumerable memories—which are unconscious unless called forth by association or request—as well as many unconscious motivations and intentions. Together, these factors constitute our identity as psychological beings.

Natural States of Awareness

We all know that our world is in continual flux. Furthermore, our own awareness of the world is not constant. We fluctuate from one state of awareness to another. Indeed, some states of awareness are not what most of us would refer to as being aware at all. While we are sleeping, for example, we are hardly aware of what is happening around us, but we are aware to some degree. Any loud noise or other abrupt stimulus will almost certainly awaken us. Even the meaning of a particular stimulus is important when we are asleep. While it may take a loud noise to awaken a normal, single adult, a new parent may be awakened by very small noises made by the baby. Somehow, we can evaluate the significance of stimuli even when asleep, and from time to time we are very much aware of dreaming. . . .

Sleep does not block our awareness; it merely alters and lessens it. Less natural or common states of awareness can be induced by hypnosis, meditation, and drugs. Certain disorders—epilepsy and the severe psychoses, for example—also can produce marked alterations in awareness.

Biological Clocks

All higher animals exhibit 24-hour activity cycles; they are more active at certain times during the 24-hour period than at others. These *biological clocks* are called *circadian rhythms* (circadian is Latin for "about a day"). Typically, predators are most active at night and sleep during the day. But some prey animals sleep at night and are active during the day. Primates, including humans and other animals that rely on vision to guide their behavior, are more likely to be active in the daytime as well as during the night. However, anyone who has passed through several time zones while flying east or west knows how difficult it can be to change from one sleep schedule to another. This "jet lag" can be so debilitating that many corporations will not allow their executives to enter negotiations for at least 2 days after such a trip. At least a week is needed to adapt to major shifts in time zones. A complete shift in the 24-hour bodily temperature cycle, which is normally lower during the night than during the day, takes even longer. In a normal individual, the temperature cycle is closely associated with the sleep cycle. We sleep during the time of the 24-hour period when our temperature is at its lowest point, usually at night.

One of the greatest mysteries about sleep is that it occurs at all. It seems to be necessary—animals die and humans often experience bizarre hallucinations if kept awake for very long periods of time—but we do not understand why. The body consumes substantially the same energy in both the quiet waking and sleep states. No known poisons or toxins require sleep in order to be dissipated. There seems to be absolutely no reason why we should sleep, yet we must.

Physiological Changes
During REM Sleep

Changes in muscle tension occur during REM sleep. These are recorded as *electromyograms (EMGs)* by electrodes that can be placed on various parts of the body but are usually put under the chin. During Stages 2, 3, and 4, EMG tracings show a high level of tension, but this tension disappears during REM periods and the chin muscles relax. Spinal reflexes also are diminished greatly. Fortunately, this greater motor inhibition during REM sleep prevents us from physically acting out our imagined activities while dreaming.

Emotional responsiveness, however, greatly increases in dreams. Besides ecstasy, surprise, terror, confusion, or erotic stimulation subjectively reported by dreamers, objective measurements also confirm that REM periods are accompanied by intense changes in the autonomic nervous system. . . . During *non-REM (NREM) sleep*, the heart regularly beats about 60 times per minute, but during REM periods it may decrease to 45 or accelerate to over 100 beats per minute in a fairly short time. Respiration can change similarly. In contrast to the regular pattern of evenly spaced breathing shown in non-REM sleep, during REM sleep dreamers often exhibit considerable variability in their breathing rate. Genital changes also occur. Males have penile erections during REM sleep about 90 percent of the time. Such erections do not occur in response to erotic dream imagery but are simply another manifestation of the wide-ranging autonomic arousal present in REM sleep. These cyclic erections occur in newborn infants and in lower animals. Females display increased lubrication and vasocongestion (increased blood flow) in the vaginal area during REM periods.

Heart and breathing rates seem to correspond to the emotional states of REM sleepers. One confirmatory technique is to wake REM sleepers and ask them to describe their dreams. REM sleepers whose breathing has been very irregular report more intense and emotional dreams than those reported after periods of regular breathing. And the same is true for heart rate. EMG activity also seems to correspond to dream content. When walking was a prominent dream activity, EMG activity increased in the leg region. When conversation was featured, EMG activity increased in the mouth region. And when an auditory emphasis occurred, the middle-ear region experienced increased EMG activity. When penile detumescence occurred before the end of a REM period, the loss of erection generally was associated with a dream report containing explicit anxiety-provoking or threatening content. These studies suggest that some general *psychophysiological parallelism* may exist in dreams. However, any exact point-for-point correspondences between specific dream imagery and associated somatic excitation remain to be discovered by future research. . . .

Imagery in REM and NREM Sleep

Scientists now know that everyone dreams and that several episodes of dreaming occur during each night of sleep. How does this dreaming unfold during the night? How does it differ from one period to another? As we begin to fall asleep and pass from drowsiness to Stage I sleep, we experience *hypnagogic imagery*. This mental activity at sleep onset usually begins with visual images of isolated geometrical shapes or kinesthetic sensations, such as floating. Two-thirds of all subjects report dreamlike content by the time they reach Stage I sleep, even though REM activity does not appear during this very brief transitional stage between wakefulness and sleep.

If subjects are awakened during their first REM period, they recall a dream about 60 percent of the time; if awakened during the second REM period, the recall level rises to 70 percent; for subsequent REM periods, the recall rate remains about 85 percent. As the night progresses, the dream reports tend to become increasingly long, vivid, and emotional. References to electrodes, the EEG machine, the experimenter, or other aspects of the laboratory setting often are incorporated into the dreams, particularly during the first few nights of sleeping in the novel laboratory situation. Waking preoccupations, such as an interest in sports, singing, or cars, may be reflected in more than one dream of a night, but no obvious linkages exist among the various dreams from a single night in terms of story plot or developing theme. A later dream does not begin where an earlier one left off.

REM reports generally contain long, emotional accounts of clearly described scenes in which several characters participate. The story line may not be connected very logically, and the events may seem implausible or even bizarre. NREM reports typically are brief and contain very little description of sensory imagery or emotionality. Subjects often claim that they could have exerted voluntary control over the events they were imagining. Subjects awakened during NREM sleep and asked if they were dreaming usually reply "no" because they were not experiencing the type of vivid mental activity common to REM sleep. If, however, they are asked, "Was anything going through your mind?" they very frequently answer "yes," adding that they were engaged in mental activity similar to thinking. If a large number of REM and NREM reports were given to judges without any indications as to the stage of sleep from which they were obtained, the judges could classify the reports with about 80 percent accuracy. The main differentiating features are that REM reports are longer and contain more visual imagery.

Why can't REM and NREM reports be discriminated with 100 percent accuracy? Because the continuum in the quality of mental imagery is not completely determined by the EEG-defined stages of sleep. The intensity and vividness of nocturnal sensory imagery also seem to be mediated by the amount of activity in the autonomic nervous system. If a person is awakened after a REM period in which eye movements have been minimal and breathing and heart rate have been regular, the report is often brief and emotionally bland. Such reports, with their lack of perceptual activities, are difficult to distinguish from NREM "thinking" reports. If a NREM awakening occurs after an interval of respiratory irregularity, the report often details a dramatic account that sounds very dreamlike. These findings suggest that REM time is not strictly dreaming time, as some authors have maintained. While most of our dreaming activity seems to occur in REM sleep, the relationship is far from an exact correspondence.

WHY DO WE SLEEP?*

"If sleep does not serve an absolutely vital function," says Allen Rechtschaffen in his book, *The Control of Sleep*, "then it is the biggest mistake the evolutionary process ever made."

The impulse to sleep is overwhelming; we spend a third of our lives doing it and feel terrible without enough. Yet after more than 25 years of research, we still are not sure of its function. Ask a number of sleep researchers the reason we sleep, and the answer you are likely to hear is, "because we get tired."

Attempts to determine why we sleep have led researchers in many different directions. At Emory University in Atlanta, Gerald Vogel has conducted studies to determine the role of rapid eye movement (REM), or dreaming, sleep in our waking behavior. One early speculation was that if REM sleep were suppressed, it would lead inevitably to psychosis. The idea, long since abandoned, was that if you suppressed REM sleep, dreams would force themselves into waking behavior and result in a kind of "dream state" similar to some forms of schizophrenia.

Vogel tried the reverse: He treated a number of clinically depressed patients by depriving them of their REM sleep for several weeks to see if their condition improved. No other drugs or treatments were used, and more than half of his patients showed significant and permanent recovery. Curiously, normal people in the study who were similarly deprived of REM sleep showed nothing more than a "REM rebound" effect signified by vivid dreaming once the REM deprivation ended.

What this suggests to Vogel is that there is some mechanism related to REM sleep that is linked to our "conscious enthusiasm." Depression may occur when something within this mechanism goes wrong, but precisely what or why remains a mystery, as does the apparent need for sleep in the first place.

Is sleep restorative? It certainly feels as if it is, but so far experiments designed to prove it have failed. Recently, researchers tried to determine if tissue restoration occurred during sleep. If so, protein, a major component of tissue, would be synthesized faster than it broke down during sleep. Precisely the opposite was found.

If restoration could not be proved directly, how about indirectly? Would the absence of sleep have serious and perhaps irreversible physiological consequences? All studies to date, which include keeping people awake for up to 12 days, indicate that nothing particularly harmful

*John Pekkanen, "Why Do We Sleep?" *Science 82*, Vol. 3, No. 4 (June, 1982) American Association for the Advancement of Science.

results. After a couple of good nights' sleep, these people feel like their old selves. In some cases, people without sleep have reported psychotic episodes, but sleep researchers believe these are caused by underlying psychological problems and not sleep deprivation itself.

Investigators have also tried to assess the role of the stages that measure sleep's depth. We know that as we grow older we sleep less deeply until we no longer reach the deepest stage at all. We also know that the pituitary gland releases growth hormone during the deepest stage. Growth hormone plays a vital role for children, but it may also be important for adults. Beginning in our mid-40s, as we sleep less and less in the deepest stage, the growth hormone release slows to a near halt. Sleep and its connection with growth hormone may be part of the larger biochemical process of aging but precisely how it interconnects is again unknown.

Two other hormones, prolactin and lutenizing hormone (LH), are also secreted during sleep. Prolactin plays an important role for nursing mothers, and LH is necessary for the production of sex hormones. But prolactin, LH, and growth hormone are secreted during wakefulness as well, though in much lesser amounts. Some as yet unknown restorative or hormonal process may occur during sleep, but it is certainly not unique.

What investigators continue to be left with are tantalizing clues, fragments of ideas that refuse to solidify into a coherent theory of why we sleep. A major obstacle is that we have not yet devised techniques sophisticated enough to probe deeply and subtly into the workings of the sleeping brain.

Many sleep researchers believe we will one day have those techniques. At present, the reason we sleep is elusive. But most researchers are betting against finding that sleep is "the biggest mistake the evolutionary process ever made."

EVERY 90 MINUTES, A BRAINSTORM*

Almost every 90 minutes while we sleep, a storm of neuronal activity erupts in the brain and bizarre dreams occur. The storm, which reflects extremely fast brain waves, lasts 20 or 30 minutes before the waves begin to slow down and the brain quiets for an hour or so. The cycle of turbulence and calm is repeated every 90 minutes throughout the night.

Sleep investigators have been familiar with these cycles for several years, but more recently, researchers have found evidence that the 90-minute cycles also continue while we are awake. Microscopic, gearlike interactions between nerve cells within the brain regulate these states of arousal, which result in a peak of mental activity every 45 minutes,

*Michael Chase, "Every 90 Minutes, A Brainstorm," Reprinted from *Psychology Today Magazine*, Copyright © 1979 Ziff-Davis Publishing Company.

followed by a trough 45 minutes later—although we do not yet know if the same nerve cells are in control during the day and night.

The cycles may help explain such phenomena as mental blocks during exams. We have all found ourselves at first unable to solve a problem, but, upon returning to it later, discover that the solution seems to pop into mind. It may be that simply waiting until the trough of the cycle passes—and tackling the problem on the upswing—permits us to find a solution. Of course, many other explanations are possible: we may have picked up clues from other questions on the exam or subconsciously worked over the problem until we hit upon an answer. Nevertheless, it is clear that we are better able to perform a variety of mental and physical tasks at regular intervals of 90 minutes or so.

Numerous tests on humans and monkeys have demonstrated that these cycles are present during waking. For example, people asked to respond to signal lights by pressing buttons generally react more quickly at 90-minute intervals. Similar cycles have been found in peaks of hunger and increased movements of the eyes during the day (other than those required by normal seeing). A male's penis becomes more tumescent every 90 minutes, on the average—a fact verified by having volunteers wear strain gauges on their penises during the day. The erections are usually accompanied by fantasies that are sometimes sexual. (Cycles range from 70 to 120 minutes in the various studies, averaging about 90 minutes.)

Studies by Daniel Kripke, a researcher at the Veterans Administration Medical Center in San Diego, suggest that people are more imaginative and fanciful every 90 minutes or so. For artists and others in creative work, it would obviously be useful to know when their peaks occur. For people like air-traffic controllers and long-distance drivers, whose jobs demand extreme concentration, it may be essential to know when they are most likely to be distracted by daydreams.

The cycles may play a particularly important role in diseased brains. For example, while both epileptic seizures and narcoleptic sleep attacks occur at different intervals and the average time between seizures and between attacks is about 90 minutes. Similarly, some schizophrenic patients apparently experience greater mental disturbance at such daily intervals.

Most data on the physiological processes affected by the cycles comes from sleep studies. In my research, I am probing the activity of single nerve cells during sleep with minute recording devices to examine the gearlike interactions between the unique neurons that maintain cycles of REM (rapid eye movement) and non-REM sleep (see "The Secret Life of Neurons," *Psychology Today*, August 1978).

While there are billions of nerve cells in the brain, it appears that very few of them actually generate sleep cycles. We know that these neurons are located in the lower portion of the brain called the brain stem; they seem to turn each other on and off in a complex fashion. For about

60 minutes after we fall asleep at night, it is assumed that certain of these neurons are active, producing a period of quiet sleep. Then, as we enter REM sleep, we believe that other neurons begin firing, setting off a chain of physiological responses in the body. Heart rate, respiration, and blood pressure fluctuate wildly, and our muscles twitch as if performing fragments of a dance led by some otherworldly conductor. Our eyes dart back and forth for about 20 or 30 minutes, until REM sleep concludes and calm returns.

What makes the sleep neurons work as they do, or why the cycles last roughly 90 minutes, we don't know. Nor do we know whether our waking cycles are due to these same neurons. We hope to find the answers to these questions by studying the electrical and chemical interactions within and between these cells.

We are only beginning to examine the intricacies of the preset clock whirring deep within the human brain. By understanding the nature of our 90-minute cycles, we may one day be able to treat brain disorders more effectively. We may also be able to take advantage of predictable increases in our mental and physical powers.

WITHOUT MY EIGHT HOURS, I'M A TYPE A*

Sleeping less than other people, and particularly getting less REM (rapid eye movement) sleep, may contribute to the hard-driving, heart attack-prone personality that psychologists call "Type A." A group of researchers at San José State University in California began investigating connections between the two when they noted the similarity between Type A characteristics and the character sketch of short sleepers drawn up by Boston psychiatrist Ernest Hartmann. Hartmann found short sleepers to be "efficient, energetic, ambitious persons who work hard and keep busy . . . [who are] sure of themselves, decisive, [self-] satisfied."

Was that Type A? Psychologists Robert A. Hicks, Robert J. Pellegrini, and James Hawkins gave more than 500 college students a sleep questionnaire and administered a form of the Jenkins Activity Survey, the measure generally used to define Type A personalities. They found that the less the students said they habitually slept, the more likely they were to report Type A Behavior.

According to earlier Hartmann counts, short sleepers form a clearly definable category of people who sleep about 20 percent less than normal subjects, and get about 25 percent less REM sleep. Short sleep thus constitutes a kind of spontaneous REM deprivation. More deliberate forms of REM deprivation are under investigation in several psychiatric centers for such therapeutic effects as bestirring deeply depressive patients. In

---

*Linda Asher, "Without My Eight Hours, I'm a Type A," Reprinted from *Psychology Today Magazine,* Copyright © 1979 Ziff-Davis Publishing Company.

several forthcoming papers, the researchers contend that REM deprivation may lead to Type-A behavior by causing increased susceptibility to stress factors: REM-deprived laboratory animals show heightened sensitivity to pain.

Both REM-deprived animals and humans tend to respond to stress with aggression, even when relaxation would be more effective. In one set of experiments, rats that would normally relax and float in a water tank swam frantically if they were short on REM sleep. Moreover, "sleep-deprived animals become fearless, taking chances and abandoning their usual self-protective behaviors," Hicks told *Psychology Today*. In experimental situations, sleep-deprived humans also lose what Hicks calls "fluid intelligence and flexibility," choosing unthinking aggressive responses to stress over more reflective alternatives.

It is unclear at this point whether short-sleeping Type A's could or should try to stretch out their REM time: the pattern that may contribute to their drive and effectiveness may also be implicated in shortening their lives.

RX FOR DEPRESSION:
A WAKE-UP CALL*

Perhaps as baffling as endogenous depression—a chronic depression that appears to result primarily from biochemical, rather than environmental, causes—are the reasons why the condition is often helped by antidepressant drugs. Some psychiatrists believe, however, that therapeutic drug action may somehow be linked to abnormalities in the chronic depressive's sleep cycle—a finding reported by a growing number of researchers (SN: 11/25/78, p. 367).

Lending considerable support to that theory are two studies reported in the March ARCHIVES OF GENERAL PSYCHIATRY. In the first, an Emory University team headed by psychiatrist Gerald W. Vogel compared the effects of rapid eye movement (REM) sleep deprivation among 14 chronic depressives and 14 non-depressed persons with insomnia. Previous studies had indicated that antidepressants somehow inhibit REM sleep, when dreaming is believed to occur.

In the first stage of the experiment, Vogel and his colleagues found that compared with the control group, depressed patients had a higher frequency and lower latency period of REM sleep, and "a new finding—an abnormal temporal distribution of REM sleep."

After depriving the subjects of REM by waking them briefly when a REM period would approach (as indicated by EEG brain wave measurements), the scientists observed improvement in the symptoms of depressed patients. Other measurements indicated that the

---

*"Rx for depression: A wake-up call," Reprinted with permission from *Science News*, the weekly news magazine of science, copyright 1980 by Science Service, Inc.

improvement could be traced to the physiological effect of the brief awakenings: Deprivation appeared at least temporarily to repair the "damaged" sleep cycle by stimulating the inborn sleep "oscillator" to operate on a relatively normal schedule. Moreover, depressed patients unresponsive to sleep deprivation were also unresponsive to the antidepressant imipramine, and significant improvement with REM deprivation occurred after about three weeks of treatment—the same period it usually takes for antidepressant drugs to become effective. The study implies some common mechanisms in "depression improvement by REM sleep deprivation and by antidepressant drugs," say the researchers.

In the second study, by university psychiatrists in Muenster, West Germany, partial sleep deprivation "significantly reduced depression symptoms" by a mean of 30 percent. The researchers reported at least some improvement in three-fourths of the 30 chronically depressed patients studied. They suggest—as does Vogel—that the process seems to involve the brain catecholamine system of neurotransmitters, which antidepressant drugs are believed to alter.

AMERICAN HABITS SURVEYED*

The results of a nine-year survey of American health habits have been released by the National Center for Health Statistics. Based on the findings, the agency has identified seven "good health habits" that

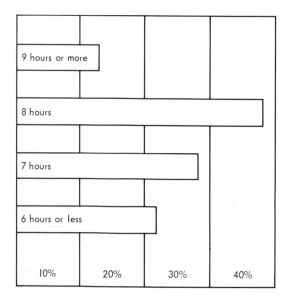

Hours of Sleep

*Reprinted by permission of GEO Magazine, August 1981, Vol. 3, p. 142.

contribute to longevity: sleeping seven to eight hours a night; eating breakfast almost every day; seldom eating snacks; keeping weight within a reasonable range (from 5 percent under to 19.9 percent over desirable levels); exercising; having fewer than five drinks at a sitting; and never smoking. People reporting six or seven of these practices were shown to enjoy better health and to live longer than those reporting fewer than four. The study found that 68 percent of white respondents slept the desired seven to eight hours a night; 61 percent of Hispanics and 56 percent of blacks did so.

WILL SLEEPING MORE HELP YOU WORRY LESS?*

True or False?

1. How long you sleep has an effect on your ability to think creatively.
2. People who sleep less worry less.
3. There are two distinct sleeper types—the early-to-bed-early-to-rise type, which psychologists term *larks*; and the later-to-bed-later-to-rise type, termed *owls*. Each type has advantages over the other.
4. Daytime sleep has a different effect on you than nighttime sleep.

Answers

1. *True.* In studies at San José State University, investigators first pretested more than 360 college students with a questionnaire on sleep habits, identifying those who for six or more months had been short sleepers (no more than six hours) or long sleepers (eight and a half hours or more), and who reported being satisfied with their sleep. Subjects were then given a test designed to assess their ability to think and reason creatively. The test contained questions such as, "What would be the result if everyone suddenly lost the ability to read and write?" Each person tested was asked to generate as many consequences as possible to the situation posed by the item in a two-minute period. Results showed that the long sleepers averaged the highest scores on the ability to think creatively. There are, of course, plenty of exceptions in the general population.
2. *False.* In further San José State University studies of personality differences between long and short sleepers, tests and interviews showed that short sleepers average significantly higher levels of worry and anxiety

*John E. Gibson, "Will Sleeping More Help You Worry Less?" Reprinted by permission of *Family Weekly*, copyright 1981, 641 Lexington Avenue, N.Y., N.Y. 10022.

than others. The findings indicated a chief source of apprehension: anxiety about how their achievements were evaluated by others.

3. *True.* And while the "owls" may have more fun getting the most mileage out of nighttime pursuits and activities, University of Florida studies of the characteristics of both types show that the "larks" have a decided edge in other departments. They were found to sleep better, were less subject to insomnia or fitful tossing and spells of wakening in the night and, as a result, awakened more rested, feeling more fit and able to face the rigors of the day than the "owls," who slept later in the morning. The "larks" were also found to have fewer physical problems, such as susceptibility to ailments and various indispositions.

4. *True.* Even the character of dreams tends to be entirely different during daytime sleep. University of California studies show that while nighttime sleep can produce dreams which are exciting, action-packed, colorful or seductively romantic, daytime sleep tends to produce dull, passive, lackluster and completely uninteresting dreams, which—if you were a sleepwalker—you'd undoubtedly walk out on. And studies conducted by a team of behavioral scientists at Italy's Universita di Trento indicate that if something that is important to be remembered is absorbed just before retiring, nighttime sleep can facilitate the recall processes, but daytime sleep did not have the same effect.

DEALING WITH TROUBLED SLEEP*

"Sometimes I know within 90 seconds if that's going to be it for the night or not; I'm up and alert, and I know that's it. . . . Other times I lie awake for 10 minutes; then the frustration sets in. I get up, go downstairs, have a jolt of coffee, and try to decide: Should I read idly, watch TV, or do something productive and get ahead of the next day?"

Robert O. Costa is describing what for him is a typical nocturnal ordeal. About three times a week, Costa, vice-president for public relations of the Hawaii Chamber of Commerce, gets up at about 2:30 a.m. after going to bed at 11 p.m. His insomnia is a sleep disorder he shares with many Americans—estimates are that anywhere from 15% to 38% of U.S. adults have problems falling or staying asleep. And insomnia is just one of the problems of troubled sleep. Some people can't breathe as they slumber, others nod off uncontrollably during the day, a few have a biological "clock" that's off. Researchers and doctors are responding by setting up sleep disorder clinics that use scientific measurement and combined therapies to help patients through their sleeping and waking hours.

Insomnia is the most common sleep-related complaint. It can take three forms: long delays in falling asleep, intermittent wakefulness during the night, and early awakening. Many cases start out as a temporary response to stress, sadness, or even intense happiness. If the sleeplessness persists for more than three weeks—because of the sufferer's personality pattern or simply because the insomnia has become a habit—doctors consider the problem to be chronic.

If you suffer from insomnia, say specialists, you may be able to improve your sleep by following "sleep-hygiene" principles. One rule, says Dr. Michael Thorpy, a neurologist and director of Montefiore Medical Center's Sleep-Wake Disorders Center in New York City, is to stay away from liquor, cigarettes, and caffeine. Liquor, especially, may be tempting because it can induce slumber initially. But as your body metabolizes the liquor, you may experience a rebound effect and wake up hours before morning. Drinking is a major contributor to insomnia; in fact, some alcoholics have disturbed sleep patterns for as long as two years after they dry out.

Cigarettes, too, are popular with insomniacs, who may not know that nicotine is a stimulant against which you cannot build a tolerance. (It differs from caffeine in that way.) Many sleepless patients, says Thorpy, tell him that "the first thing they do is put on the light and have a cigarette." Yet in studies conducted by Dr. Anthony Kales, of the Hershey (Pa.) Sleep Research & Treatment Center of Pennsylvania State University, nonsmokers were observed to be better sleepers than smokers were, and smokers' sleep improved as soon as they stopped smoking.

Another habit to quit, say sleep specialists, is the long-term use of sleeping pills, called "hypnotics." For one thing, they act much like liquor once in the system—when they wear off during sleep, you may experience "rebound insomnia" that can be more intense than your pre-pill sleepless-ness. If you decide to stop taking these medications, though, do so slow-ly and under a physician's guidance. Quick or careless withdrawal can have serious consequences, including seizures.

One thing you are encouraged to ingest is a light meal before bedtime, something bland such as milk and a sandwich. Milk—along with beef, eggs, and cheddar cheese—contains L-tryptophan, an amino acid that, some researchers say, may help get you to sleep. Thorpy and Kales do not feel that L-tryptophan is a significant aid for insomniacs, but they approve of the bedtime snack, which, they say, can be soothing and can promote drowsiness.

A long-term exercise program can improve sleep, too. But don't expect results right away, and don't exercise for up to three hours before you turn in, since exercise increases the rate of your heartbeat and adrenalin levels. When you do turn in, preferably at about the same time every night, make sure you feel sleepy. Going to bed earlier to try to make up for your insomnia doesn't work, since it's almost impossible to sleep when you're not tired. It's easier to stave off fatigue than to try to sleep hours before your bedtime.

Another time to stay out of bed, or off an office couch, is during the day. No naps. Napping throws off your sleep-wake pattern, which, if you're like most insomniacs, is more than a bit erratic. Once you're in bed, turn out the light and try to sleep. Don't read, watch TV, do a crossword puzzle, or talk on the phone. It's important to condition your responses to think of time in bed as time sleeping, says Thorpy, who forbids his insomniac patients to do anything in bed but sleep. (There is one exception: making love.) Counting sheep, relaxation techniques, anything that will keep you from actually thinking and worrying can help, as can a "sleep-sound" machine, a device about 6 in. by 4 in. that "hums" soothingly and screens out noise.

If you try all this and you still can't sleep, or if you wake up early and can't get back to sleep, get out of bed after 15 minutes. Leave the room and read something slightly boring or watch TV—preferably something as bland as your bedtime snack. Don't tackle work you've taken from the office. As soon as you are drowsy, try going to bed again.

These techniques may not be enough for you. If that's the case, you might want to consult a doctor or a sleep disorder specialist. There are now about 100 reputable sleep disorder centers in the U. S. Each uses a team approach. Staffs typically include a neurologist, psychiatrist, psychologist, cardiologist, and otolaryngologist (an ear, nose, and throat doctor). After taking a thorough medical, psychological, and social history and conducting extensive physical and psychological examinations, the team will create an individualized treatment program for you. A major diagnostic tool at the center is the polysomnogram, which is an all-night recording of your sleep, breathing, heart activity, and limb movements. It can be used along with a closed-circuit camera and a microphone if the doctors want to see and hear you sleep, as well. A routine PSG results in about 1,500 pages of data. If you are a candidate for a PSG, you spend one or two nights at a center hooked up with wires and electrodes so you can be monitored all night. (The cost at Montefiore's center is $450 per polysomnogram; insurance reimbursement varies, so check your policy first.) In two weeks you get the results of the monitoring and of your physical and psychological exams.

The treatment prescribed will be individualized. It may include psychotherapy or the use of hypnotics for a very short period, just long enough to get you out of the "habit" of insomnia. If the tests show, for example, that you are sleepless because you have a "circadian" sleep-wake disorder, which means your biological clock tells you to sleep during the day and stay up at night, you may be treated with "chronotherapy." Chronotherapy advances your bedtime by a few hours a day for some weeks (or months) until you reach a normal sleep-wake pattern. You and the team select a "new" bedtime that is best for you, taking into consideration your biological rhythms and your work schedule.

Treatment is also available if the polysomnogram indicates that your sleeplessness is triggered by "nocturnal myoclonus." This condition, in which leg spasms occur every 20 to 40 seconds for periods lasting up to an hour, results in constant, if brief, arousals from sleep. Medications can be prescribed to treat nocturnal myoclonus.

Daytime Sleepiness

Although insomnia is the most common sleep problem, the majority of people who resort to sleep disorder clinics do not go because of insomnia. They complain instead of excessive daytime sleepiness. Two ailments can be involved in this. One is sleep apnea, or difficulty in breathing while asleep.

Apnea has two forms. In central apnea, a neurological problem, the lungs are strangely paralyzed during sleep. Victims must become at least semiconscious to breathe. They may not remember waking up, but they complain of overwhelming fatigue during the day. Central apnea is most often treated with medications, assisted-ventilation devices, and rarely, with a tracheotomy—a surgical procedure that creates a permanent hole in the neck so air can go directly into the windpipe and lungs. During the day, the patient wears a plastic "cork" over the hole, which a shirt collar hides easily. The cork allows normal daytime breathing and is removed at night to allow sufficient breathing during sleep.

The second type of apnea, obstructive sleep apnea, is a condition where the upper airway is blocked during sleep, cutting off air to the lungs. Sufferers may wake up as often as 500 times a night, and family members will often report "snoring that is heard rooms away," says Dr. Aaron Sher, an otolaryngologist who works with Montefiore's Thorpy. Bedmates may also mention a pattern of normal sleep, loud snoring, gasping, and frequent awakenings.

The typical victim of obstructive sleep apnea—an overweight man in his mid-40s to mid-50s—may fall asleep frequently during the day. For Richard Zimmerman, a 30-year-old owner of a New Jersey office-supply company, symptoms began six years ago. "It started with falling asleep while I was driving," he says. A doctor "told me I was burning my candle at both ends. So I went to bed earlier. It didn't help." Then he noticed some nighttime symptoms. "I would wake up needing to breathe. Sometimes I'd get up and walk around the bed to get to the bathroom, all without breathing." A second doctor diagnosed him correctly but treated him with medication that failed to correct the ailment. Finally, a neurologist prescribed a visit to Montefiore's sleep center. At Montefiore, a complete history and a polysomnogram confirmed the diagnosis. Sher treated Zimmerman with a new surgical procedure—only two have been performed so far at Montefiore—that was pioneered at the Henry Ford Hospital Sleep Disorders & Research Center in Detroit. The surgery, called a UPP (for uvulo-palato-pharyngoplasty), involves enlarging the space around the mouth and upper throat by removing excess folds of tissue and performing "a sort of facelift of the throat," says Sher.

The operation behind him, Zimmerman has a tracheotomy, which will be closed after the Montefiore team is satisfied that he can sleep well without the hole in his neck. He is quite pleased with the results: "The difference is that I get up once, or never, during the night," he says, adding: "I'm back on the road, driving and visiting customers, which I had stopped doing." And, he reports, "I don't snore anymore; my wife loves it."

If left untreated, apnea can be quite dangerous. Because it results in less oxygen intake, and therefore low oxygen levels in the blood, the condition can lead to heart problems. Children with obstructive apnea may develop congestive heart failure, although removal of tonsils and adenoids can sometimes correct a child's sleep apnea.

Emotionally Triggered Slumber

Harder to correct is narcolepsy, the other sleep disorder connected to excessive daytime sleep. About 200,000 Americans suffer from this neurological ailment, in which sleep suddenly overtakes a waking person. The instant sleep is usually accompanied by cataplexy—a weakness of limbs or trunk muscles—and is frequently triggered by strong emotions. Each attack lasts about five minutes. When victims of narcolepsy try to sleep at night, they may have frightening hallucinations, as well as paralysis that lasts for two to three minutes. Treatment includes the use of drugs, usually stimulants.

The new specialists are optimistic about curing—or at least easing—every sleep-related problem. To locate specialists at a sleep disorder center near you, write to the Association of Sleep Disorders Centers, P.O. Box YY, East Setauket, N.Y., 11733. At Montefiore, says Thorpy, "our clinical impression is that we can help virtually everyone we see."

WHY PILLS ARE BECOMING PASSÉ*

Insomniacs take two types of medications to try to induce sleep: over-the-counter (nonprescription) drugs, in which the main ingredient is antihistamine, and prescribed pills, mostly those classed as "benzo-diazepines."

*Reprinted from the October 11, 1982 issue of *Business Week* by special permission, © 1982 by McGraw-Hill, Inc., N.Y., N.Y. 10020. All rights reserved.

Very little independent research has been conducted to test the efficacy of OTC drugs, but at least one study found them to be relatively ineffective. Antihistamines promote no more than drowsiness, and manufacturers of these drugs are careful to describe their products only as "sleep aids."

These sleep aids can have serious side effects. A 1979 report issued by the Institute of Medicine, part of the National Academy of Sciences, states that although fatal overdoses are rare, these drugs can cause confusion, disorientation, and memory disturbances. Moreover, antihistamines repress the sleep stage associated with dreaming. Withdrawing from the drugs after regular use can temporarily intensify your dreaming and produce nightmares.

Slow market. Last year, Americans spent about $30.5 million on sleep aids, but their popularity may be waning. Allen Mercill, a vice-president of the Proprietary Assn., which represents manufacturers of OTC products, says that the market for these drugs is now stagnant.

Prescribed sleeping pills, referred to as "hypnotics," are also being used less frequently. Prescriptions for all but one type of benzodiazepine —flurazepam (Dalmane)—have declined by about 40% since 1971. Benzodiazepines, considered somewhat safer than barbiturates, were orginally marketed to relax muscles and to relieve anxiety. Valium, for example, is a benzodiazepine.

"Most people in the sleep field avoid the use of hypnotics," says Dr. Michael Thorpy, director of Montefiore Medical Center's Sleep-Wake Disorders Center in New York. When they are prescribed, it is for a short time only, to break a patient's cycle of sleeplessness.

For one thing, most benzodiazepines stay in your system for just a few hours. Once your body metabolizes them during sleep, you can experience "rebound insomnia" that is more serious than your pre-pill sleeplessness.

Diminished driving skills. The few hypnotics that stay in the body longer can create potentially serious side effects in the daytime. They may, for example, diminish your driving skills. And since all benzodiazepines, even those that act only briefly, are dangerous when combined with alcohol, patients who take the long-acting variety—flurazepam, for example—must avoid liquor for a few days after they take their last pill.

All hypnotics depress breathing functions somewhat, so they are particularly dangerous for people with sleep-related respiratory ailments. Anyone with liver disease should avoid them, too, as should pregnant women: Limited evidence has linked them with birth disorders. Finally, some studies have demonstrated that chronic use of hypnotics only makes insomnia worse.

Nevertheless, doctors wrote more than 31 million prescriptions for sleeping pills in 1980. The Institute of Medicine reports that physicians' information about dosage and side effects of the drugs came not from researchers but primarily from drug salespeople, journal advertising, and the *Physician's Desk Reference*, sources considered incomplete or questionable by the IOM, whose report concluded: "It is difficult to justify much of the current prescribing of sleep medication."

STUDENT ESSAY: SLEEP-TYPES

"Early to bed and early to rise makes a man healthy, wealthy and wise" is an adage accorded to Benjamin Franklin. In today's world of working long hours many men and women fit into this pattern of early to bed and early to rise. Did you ever feel that this philosophy makes you healthy, wealthy, but too tired to enjoy life? All human beings share the need for sleep, yet individual sleep patterns are varied; and it has been said that one's personality may be related to the number of hours one sleeps each night.

The person who sleeps four hours a night is a nervous, high-strung individual. She is a very light sleeper and awakens at the slightest disturbance. If you have ever slept with this type, you know she generally tosses and turns all night. Peter Farb, in his essay, "The Rhythms and Levels of Sleep" would say this person never reaches a deep sleep because of her almost conscious state. During REM the person is usually restless. (This is the opposite of N-REM where body movements are minimal.) The basic lack of sleep makes this person a bumbling wreck. Usually hyperactive, she has trouble trying to relax. According to Farb, lack of REM causes memory loss and poor test performance. If you are like her, you may need tranquilizers to calm your nerves. This person probably became this way by living next to a fire whistle.

The six-hour sleeper is often very irritable. He is the type of person who will yell at you without a reason. This person is generally a workaholic and very ambitious, usually to the point of driving you up the wall. The short sleep period he receives causes him to be emotionally irritable. According to Farb, irritability is related to the shorter amount of REM sleep obtained which is enough to cause mild repercussions, such as forgetfulness, stress, and low resistance to emotional trauma. If you know this type of person, beware, for he is a tiger. If you *are* this person, God help you. One most likely becomes this way from being dropped as a child.

An eight-hour sleeper has an even temperament and is usually good-natured. He is much less irritable than both the four-hour or six-hour sleeper because he gets more REM sleep. He tends to be more energetic. And girls, if you are out on a date with him, watch out! The eight-hour sleep period is a good duration of time, about five and one-half sleep cycles, according to Farb's essay. Eight hours seems to be just enough for you to have a good memory and the right temperament to handle traumatic situations. For example, on the average, an eight-hour sleeper will, according to Farb's rule, handle a death in the family better than a six-hour sleeper. He most likely developed this sleeping habit and good temperament from being sung to as a child.

You might have a problem talking to a ten-hour sleeper because it is hard to imagine her up long enough to hold a conversation. She tends to have a good memory and to be very stable mentally. She is very hard to wake up in the morning because after staying in bed so long her body thinks she died. She probably became this way because her alarm never went off. Her sleep pattern shows that she receives a lot of REM and N-REM which are vital to her physical and mental well-being. If you are not a ten-hour sleeper, avoid a relationship with someone of this nature. You can never plan to do anything before noon.

Farb states that "...sleep had long been thought to be a time of quiescence, not one in which the brain was actively generating movement...." However, this hypothesis has been dispelled by further research into the subject. The amount of sleep one gets is a major factor in one's life. In addition, did you know that on the average you spend 1/3 of your life sleeping? This means that you sleep eight hours a night, as the vast majority of people do. However, if you fall into one of the other three categories, you might follow some of the previously described patterns. Of course it is not conclusive that the amount of sleep you receive is the only factor affecting your habits, but it can contribute to your personality. Thus, only after you have made your own experiments and discovered how much sleep you need can you categorize yourself into a particular sleeping type. When you get into bed tonight, just before you turn off the light, remember, all human beings share the need for sleep and the amount you get may affect your personality.

Index